EXPAT:

Leaving the USA for Good

Bruce H. Joffe

EXPAT:

Leaving the USA for Good

Bruce H. Joffe

This book is dedicated to my children, Jonah and Jen, for theirs is the future in a complex, changing, and (sometimes) conspiratorial world.

Also by Bruce H. Joffe:

My Name Is Heretic:
Reforming the Church, from Guts to Glory

The Gospel According to Facebook:
Social Media and the Good News

Personal PR:
Public Relations and Marketing Tips that Work to Your
Advantage

Square Peg in a Round Hole

A Hint of Homosexuality?
Gay and Homoerotic Imagery in American Print
Advertising

The Scapegoat

"Perhaps there was something 'rotten in Denmark,' in his own life, or in the life of his society and it smelled. Maybe it was more than just dull; perhaps Abraham felt as if he was caught in a cesspool. Or perhaps his old life was oppressive, constrained, hemmed in. Perhaps it was filled with unnecessary social misery. Maybe he felt so hemmed in that, sometimes, he couldn't even breathe. Or perhaps his old life was filled with yearning, an ache for something more. Yearning for another land, another way of being. That feeling of perhaps being full, but still hungry.

"Are we going to remain in the world of the dull, the repetitive, the same ole, same ole ... or are we, like Abraham, going to respond to that voice that invites us to leave our old way of being and enter a life beyond convention and our domestications of reality? The voice speaks of promise to us, 'I will show you a better way, a better country.'"

Marcus Borg
Days of Awe and Wonder

Obviously, these are just my personal observations and some may be skewed or faulty. Nonetheless, we believe ourselves better off now because of these differences that teach us to value the customs of one country – and its culture – even when compared to another.

Please note that the information shared here is based on our own experiences and observations ... which take into account the province, city, and village where we live.

I share this to be helpful in planning, not contentious, and appreciate your open-minded understanding.

Greener Pastures?

"At your age, isn't it about time that you stopped moving around from place to place, seeking greener pastures? Why can't you just stay put and settle down somewhere … ?"

With words like these, I have been challenged by people I know – who assume they know me – about the nomadic quality that apparently defines my quixotic travels, seeking and reaping fullness in life.

# # # # #

I came of age in New York City, graduating secondary school and then earning my Bachelor's degree at a state university on Long Island. Excelling at Spanish, I worked at a veterinary hospital and in a supermarket to afford spending the summer following my high school graduation – and, later, much of my undergraduate studies – in Spain.

Back in the States, I served (briefly) as an interpreter at the United Nations and then as a public school Spanish teacher. During those years, I earned a Master's degree in Education and a Ph.D. in Business Communication.

My salary no longer was earned by teaching Spanish, but by working as a college professor … a public relations specialist … and a writer/actor on several daytime soap operas.

In between, I studied theology at a Northern Virginia seminary.

Later, I met my partner in life, with whom I have been blessed for more than 25 years now. We moved from my former residence to a charming townhouse nearby. As my earnings increased and investing in real estate beckoned as a road to financial security, we sold the townhouse and moved into larger quarters where we lived for several years, until we decided to downsize and move to an upscale townhouse—still in Manassas, Virginia.

The combination of 9/11 and watching too much HGTV convinced us to sell our Washington-area townhouse and take on a major renovation of an historic property in Mount Jackson, a town in Virginia's Shenandoah Valley. As CEO of my company and a faculty member of the state university system – combined with the expansive possibilities of the Internet – "place" no longer was as important as "possibilities."

Professional potential took us from Virginia to Wisconsin ... from Wisconsin to Jacksonville, Florida ... from Jacksonville back to Staunton, Virginia, in the Shenandoah Valley ... and then onto "retirement" in Sturgeon Bay, Wisconsin.

I continued to teach (online) and preach from a progressive pulpit.

# # # # #

Fast forward digression ...

About ten years ago, we purchased a small "vacation bolt" in a typical town in southern Spain, where we've spent months each year enjoying a different way of life. Last year, we added a property in Portugal where we now live—about a six-hour drive, door-to-door, from our home in Spain.

On March 25, 2018, we departed our country of birth to live in another.

We no longer reside in the USA, but divide our time now between our primary house in Lousa, Castelo Branco, Portugal and our home-away-from-home in southern Spain. Yet we still are citizens of the United States and care (cringe?) deeply about what's happening there. And we have chosen — deliberately — not to be barraged day and night with all the atrocities, crimes, and conflicts of the Trump administration which had divided the country, estranged families, stolen from the people, alienated us from our allies, poisoned our environment, and brought us

2

time and again to the brink of unthinkable disasters and carnage.

# # # # #

My heart continues to cry for the beloved country and I will express disgust and rage at those who purportedly represent us but actually profit and privilege from their perches.

No, I don't regret the moves we made.

All things considered, our lives have been enriched by knowing people from all walks of life throughout the United States and around the world. Social media conveniently bring many together, enabling us to cross-pollinate the people and places we've known over the past 50+ years: John Bowne High School classmates, SUNY Stony Brook alumni, and dearly beloved friends in Manassas, Mt. Jackson, Staunton, Racine, Jacksonville, Sturgeon Bay, Spain, and Portugal.

We now face challenges of a different sort here in Portugal, the world's third most peaceful country (following Iceland and New Zealand) and, reportedly, the friendliest one—especially to expats.

In essence, we must start from scratch – finding friends, doctors, dentists, veterinarians, hair cutters, food, and our way around – all in a language we don't yet speak or quite understand. We need to learn how to slow down, how to enjoy the simplest pleasures of life, and to trust that tomorrow will bring its own promises and priorities.

Thank you for taking part in our journey. After all, it's not the destination – but how we get there – that matters most.

Getting Going

"Get going, already," motioned the young couple who had purchased our house in Sturgeon Bay, Wisconsin, and were waiting, eagerly, for us to depart from what was now to be their new home.

In addition to our house, they had bought a good deal of our furniture — as well as my favorite toy, an all-wheel drive Jaguar.

We had disposed of most of our possessions and keepsakes.

Except for the contents of one 8 x 8 x 20 foot shipping container filled with an assortment of "household goods" and our beloved artwork, collected and curated together over 25+ years together (plus not too few U-Haul "wardrobe" boxes filled with blankets, comforters, bed linens, towels, and other household goods that we'd purchased for donation to the needy in Portugal—especially victims of the fires), everything else we owned, including Russ's Jeep Grand Cherokee, had been sold, gifted to loved ones, or donated to nonprofit charities.

Turning back one last time to wave a final good-bye, I realized that we had divested much, if not most, of the content comprising our life in the United States, as we prepared to make the one-way journey to Portugal with our three dogs, three large suitcases, and two allotted carry-on bags containing computers, passports, and other essentials.

Over the past ten years, we had been fortunate and privileged to own "vacation bolts" in Spain and/or Portugal, and to travel there once or twice annually, enjoying a month to six weeks during each visit.

But this time would be different.

It wasn't a visit. We'd be staying, not returning.

One-way, not round-trip, tickets.

This was the first time we were traveling with our dogs, three miniature schnauzers, who'd accompany us in the cabin on the three flights taking us to our new home: Green Bay > Chicago, Chicago > Philadelphia, and

4

Philadelphia > Madrid (where we would rent a car large enough to transport our family and assorted paraphernalia on the four-hour drive to our property in Lousa, a tiny town on the outskirts of Castelo Branco, the nearest major metropolis to the Spanish border).

Endlessly, we had talked about living in Europe alongside other the expats – from the UK and the Netherlands, Australia, Canada, Sweden and elsewhere – who had become part and parcel of our family and circle of friends in Spain and, later, in Portugal.

But they were European Union nationals. Different rules applied to them than applied to us. Even the Brits, though fearful of potential consequences their "Brexit" might cause, were convinced they would never be forced to leave the countries to which they had emigrated. Certainly, protections and provisions would be included in the terms and conditions negotiated during the UK's exit from the EU.

For our part, we loved the lifestyle we lived in Spain and Portugal. Life was easier (or easy-going) and slower there. Far cheaper, too. And healthier. We walked rather than drove most days; typically, we ate less but healthier; and we drank far more red wine. As a "mañana mentality" took hold, we felt far less stressed and much more liberated. All in all, our quality of life greatly surpassed our cost of living.

Yet ...

Visits and vacations are different from full-time living and residence. So, we dawdled, too comfortable in our intimacies and surroundings to actually make such a major move.

Perhaps it was the regular, routine Social Security payments I had worked a lifetime to earn. More probably, however, the political changes – first subtle, then crassly overt – which had changed the climate of our country, provided the real motivation for us to get going and relocate.

# # # # #

Since my public school days, I'd seen a president assassinated, the murder of his assassin, and the death of his assassin's assassin … all reported by the media, often "live" on our black and white TVs;

Later, I saw that same president's brother assassinated as he, too, campaigned to become our country's number one man;

I'd seen a Democrat – from Texas yet! – inherit the presidency, but decide not to seek another term because we had become so deeply entrenched in a war triggering marches on Washington and uprisings at campuses across the country (where students were shot dead by "first responders");

I'd seen a president and his vice-president, both disgraced by scandals, resign from the two highest offices in the land;

I'd seen our first "unelected" president, when a congressman – but not the Speaker of the House – succeeded his predecessors;

I'd seen a well-meaning peanut farmer from Georgia elected president, a decent and truly Christian man, relegated to the back burners of history … remembered more for his brother's beer than his own accomplishments (which finally are being realized and accredited);

I'd seen a beloved, second-rate actor become president and be shot (along with others) in front of our televised eyes … and, yet, despite the outcry, no real gun controls were effected;

I'd seen a father and son each elected president—the first for a single term, the second for two;

I'd seen a president selected by a partisan Supreme Court when the votes were so close and the election errors so many that day after day, week after week, a "winner" still couldn't be called;

I'd seen a likable boomer – one of my own generation – impeached while in office because of alleged improprieties dealing with questionable real estate transactions and this president's penchant for women, including consensual sex with a young intern whose stained, blue dress immortalized the evidence of his infidelities;

I'd seen the first black man elected President of the United States, yet denied his rightful responsibilities during eight years of impasse with a do-nothing Congress;

And I'd seen the first woman nominated to be our country's commander-in-chief … only to be trumped, trounced, and toppled by a lying, cheating, hateful, tax-evading, bankrupt, conflicted con man who had become a "brand" that abused and took advantage of people, denouncing them daily with tweets and promoting a helter-skelter agenda of favoritism to the rich.

Flabbergasted, flustered, and furious, I began asking everyone who'd listen a series of "since when" questions.

Since when:

• Did the executive branch of our government become so authoritarian that the legislature cowers instead of confronting the mess (or rushes off to retire with its ill-begotten gains and lifetime pensions)?

• Did members of Congress become "leaders" of this country, rather than representatives of the people who elected them … as if we were mere pawns in some preconceived, haphazard game of high stakes chess or roller-skating championships?

• Did it become all right for nepotism to be an acceptable way of governing this country, where non-credentialed family members wheel and deal with emissaries from foreign countries for personal gain right there on site in the White House?

• Did it become legitimate for subordinate staff and aides to claim "executive privilege" and refuse to testify before Congress and/or its designated special investigators?

• Did we become a people who cheer – whose religious leaders bless – malicious, slanderous, hateful, and divisive words of a toxic, laughingstock president and his henchmen?

- Did our country stand alone, apart from the rest of the world (especially our allies and trading partners), in such critical matters as climate change, first-strike warfare, trade wars and economic tariffs ... all based on the nonsensical ramblings of one man whose ignorance is only surpassed by his ego and arrogance?
- Did we have such a revolving door of executive and administrative staff – ambassadors, advisers, agency heads, justice officials – coming and going ... due, in large measure, to firings or their fear of being associated with criminals and/or criminal offenses?
- Did responsible statesmen so deliberately ignore and refuse to investigate multiple alleged crimes and charges of injustice against a lifetime judicial nominee, so as to effectively rush through the confirmation of a new justice with dubious standards and questionable morality? Especially when that judge will serve as jurist in a potential trial of high crimes and misdemeanors (including treason) committed by the man who nominated him?
- Did our principal international nemesis (Russia) become a country whose leaders and politics are coddled and colluded ... or where independent "back channels" between the Kremlin and White House are surreptitiously planned by players from both regimes?
- Did our government cater exclusively to the richest 1% of the country, while denying the other 99% even scraps from the banquet table?
- Did the administration in power benefit and take so much in personal pursuits and paranoid pleasures ... a country whose president spends one-third of his time playing golf, a third tweeting or watching TV, and another third grand-standing before his base?
- Did it become legal to ambush trillions of dollars in new debt a year for tax cuts to appease the already privileged and patrons ... only to warn that Social Security, Medicare, and other government programs we were required to pay into must be minimized?
- Did our chief executive dedicate himself with such glee

to so swiftly and unilaterally dismantling myriad social welfare and infrastructure programs that guided and protected our people, basically to strike his predecessor president?

• Did it become acceptable to acknowledge – without corrective measures – that more than two-thirds of what a president says are proven lies?

• Did money so effectively dictate the rules of the realm, rather than the voices and votes of the people?

• Did the legitimate, mainstream press – always considered the fourth pillar of our government – degenerate into an "enemy of the people" … while hurried and bizarre social media platforms became the pedestals for fake news and alternative realities?

• Did we end becoming a melting pot of diversity, benefiting from the talents and hard work of immigrants seeking to contribute to a better life?

• Did democracy die in the USA?

# # # # #

Since when did all these heinous things happen in a country birthed by liberty, freedom, and justice for all?

When?

Since November 2016, when Donald Trump was anointed president and commander-in-chief of this hitherto generous, gallant, compassionate country ... although some will maintain that planning for much of this usurping had been long in the making—by a complicit Congress, curtailed court system, and conspiring officials, whose patrons pull their (purse) strings ... to divert attention from their back room back-stabbing. And by too many people who should know better, but prefer to gloat in their deplorable despair and disdain.

We lived in a place and time where – by and large – our elected representatives are beholden to their patrons, rather than to their constituents. They answer to no one (except themselves and their keepers) and exempt themselves from the rules that they make.

We lived in a place and time where the disparity between the income of corporations and their executives is radically beyond the grasp of working people. And, yet, despite all the loot the rich have accumulated and stashed, it's not enough.

So, our Congress is intent on denying the safety nets ordinary people depend on, while giving even more money to those hoarding what they already have.

We lived in a place and time where our legitimate mainstream media, hitherto the bastion of freedom and justice, have been summarily dismissed and replaced with alternative facts, truths, and realities. Bloggers and slanted nonsense are held in the same regard as our responsible press.

We lived in a place and time where political gerrymandering has corrupted our Electoral College such that twice – twice! – within a generation, the people's choices for president were overruled and citizens denied their right to vote.

We lived in a place and time where we are isolated from the rest of the world, often the brunt of its jokes. We're the only nation in the world not to sign on to global environmental protection agreements and accords. We've vacated our promises to trade with, protect, and support other countries (which now question whether we can be trusted anymore).

We lived in a place and time where moneyed people against public education, investment people who caused our near financial collapse, opportunistic people who inflated the prices of critical medicines, energy executives who knew naught about diplomacy, hunting advocates, and people whose memories failed them on imperative legal matters, are now running the very government offices they had hijacked … but scientists and otherwise knowledgeable people are forbidden to speak truth to power.

We lived in a place and time where a destructive,

conflicted, ignorant, narcissistic, self-serving, delusional, degenerate believes he's entitled to follow his own misguided interpretations of the words enshrined in our Constitution and other guiding documents. And that his own, private businesses should benefit from the country's public business.

We lived in a place and time where some of us sign petitions, write letters to editors, make telephone calls, knock on doors, use every technological advantage to speak our hearts and minds, march on occasion, gather for community and committee meetings ... but our representatives decline to address us, collectively, in meetings.

Indeed, we lived in a desperate place and time.

What kind of desperate measures, if any, should we be taking?

Each must do what we believe best, according to our own particular situations, strategies, and peculiar circumstances.

For us, the decision was to leave.

We will always consider ourselves American citizens, cast our votes in USA elections, and care about the land where we were borne.

But to intake and inhale this poisonous venom, a contagious cancer that has spread across the United States and, through it, the world?

No!

Internalizing the strife, we were grief-stricken, mentally exhausted, spiritually drained, and physically disabled.

The time had come for us to move on ...

We would move from the USA to Europe as expats.

Pluperfect or Past Perfect?

Professor and pastor probing the intersection of media, religion, gender, and other cultural norms.

These words inscribed on Facebook, LinkedIn, and other social media sites profile how I imagine myself.

So, there: now you know enough about me.

Reading between the lines, however, would inform you that we had moved around the USA quite a bit – living in New York, Virginia, Maryland, Wisconsin, Florida – as career changes and professional opportunities beckoned. Fluent in Spanish, I traveled throughout Mexico, South and Central America, as a liaison for international adoption agencies.

As mentioned, *mi marido* and I had long considered living in another country and experiencing a different culture. Learning a new language to converse and communicate, we believed, was an admirable goal. Some people are so defensive of their own ways and means that their sense of identity and nationalism is threatened when other ways are engaged in and embraced.

With credentials from the University of Madrid, a vacation bolt in Andalucía, and a growing circle of friends there, Spain seemed a natural first choice for us. But the process of applying for and being granted retirement residency in Spain can be onerous and demanding at best, next to impossible at worst.

Many countries of the European Union are also part of what's known as the "Schengen" zone. The same Schengen application form is used to apply for residency in any of its 22 EU nations. But the interpretations of myriad functional requirements often vary from country to country.

Take finances, for example.

All Schengen countries want to know that you have the financial means to provide adequately for yourself and your dependents, without being a burden on the country and its economy. All countries seek proof that you have the necessary wherewithal—albeit from Social Security, other pensions and annuities, investments and savings, bank accounts, even credit immediately available via "charge" cards.

Spain dictates specific annual earnings expected retirees must receive: "The minimum income required is 400% of the IPREM (Public Income Index) annually plus the required percentage per each additional family member." At the time, that meant, for a retirement visa and residency in Spain, one was expected to receive no less than $2,500 per month or $30,000 a year. Add $7,500 more for each dependent.

Wow!

How many Spaniards – especially those living in small towns throughout the country – earn that kind of money? Very, very few! For a country where the cost of living is so relatively low, I maintain Spain is shooting itself in the foot by requiring such high-income levels from prospective retirees who would likely support the economy by spending money on their homes, food, and lots of leisure time activities.

Consider Portugal, now: €14,000 annually is an approximated income you have to make to get a "D7" residency visa in Portugal. But it can change depending on the number of "dependents" (wife, children, etc.). That amount is basically considered 100% of the minimum wage (MW) required for the husband/or wife (the visa's owner) + 50% of the MW for his wife/her husband. For each child, it's 30% of the MW. Portugal's 2018 monthly minimum wage was 580 euros.

Unless it has changed, financial means or financial subsistence in Portugal doesn't require proof of income, simply proof of access to funds. Savings, bank accounts, investment funds, etc., all count as money to which you have access.

"You can qualify for permanent residency in Portugal simply by showing a reliable minimum income of at least 1,100 euros per month," *U.S. News & World Report* reported in a May 9, 2017 article. "This program is not intended specifically for retirees and is open to anyone. You can apply and qualify at any age, and the income you show can be earned or passive."

In other words, money in banks … savings and retirement accounts … investments … even a line of credit on your "charge" card will count towards meeting your financial means in Portugal, as long as you have access to the money. The same holds true in many other EU countries: Italy and France are particularly popular, among others.

The process of applying for the right to reside in a Schengen EU country includes completing and/or acquiring much time-consuming paperwork, lots of patience, and more money than might be imagined. Included among the documents (some only available for a fee) required to be submitted with the official visa application: Original passport, a copy of the passport, and another accepted form of identification (driver's license, state ID, or voter's registration card). Plus a copy of this. A notarized document explaining why you are requesting the visa … the purpose, place, and length of your stay (and any other reasons you need to explain). Proof of permanent retirement income from an official institution (social security and/or private source) to live without working. Proof of accommodation: either a lease or title deed of property you own. Proof of other sources of income or properties (if applicable). Proof of health insurance with full coverage, necessarily including repatriation coverage. Criminal History Information/ Police Background Check, which must be verified by fingerprints. It cannot be older than three months from the application date. The certificate must be issued from either the State Department(s) of Justice or from every state you've lived in during the past five years. This document must then be legalized with the Apostille of the Hague Convention by the corresponding Secretary of the State. Alternatively, FBI Records, issued by the U.S. Department of Justice and legalized with the Apostille of the Hague Convention by the U.S. Department of State in Washington, DC, are acceptable. (A local police background check will not be accepted; but you must also get a police record from the countries where you have lived during the last five years.) A recent doctor's statement signed by the physician on the physician's or medical center's letterhead (not older than three months) indicating that you have been examined and found free of any contagious diseases according to the International Health Regulation 2005. Married? Your spouse must submit the same documents as you, together with a marriage certificate (original, issued in the last six months, plus a photocopy). Minor children must also submit the same documents as the applicant, along with original birth certificates issued in the last twelve months ... and a photocopy.

Quite a list, huh? But, that's only the beginning!

For Spain, every document submitted must be translated into Spanish ... and not just by anyone. Only "certified" translators identified – many of whom charge $40 per page to translate – are acceptable. Despite being fluent in Spanish and having taught the language for quite a few years, I wasn't on the list and couldn't do our own translations.

But, for us, the real sticking point was the annual retirement income requirement. We owned (without a mortgage) our home in Spain and could live quite comfortably in our small town on my monthly Social Security payments. Nonetheless, $1,700 per month supplemented by a $250 private annuity didn't come close to the $2,500 Spain required. Especially not when factoring in Russ as my spousal dependent.

We could enjoy visiting Spain twice each year for up to 90 days per visit when separated by 180 days ... but we couldn't live there full-time.

# # # # #

I will always admire Canada and respect the Canadian social contract with its people. But I wouldn't want to live there. Wisconsin has been cold enough for us. Delving into international retirement trends, we learned that many Canadians owned property in Mexico, where they retreated, if possible, to escape the blustery cold.

So, next, we looked into Mexico as a potential retirement haven. But the stories about traveling through Mexico – especially around towns near the U.S. border – were chilling in a different way: the fear factor. Americans inadvertently (but sometimes deliberately) had been targets of drug cartels and other criminals in the country.

We considered the Lake Chapala and Ajiic areas outside Guadalajara – known for its "ideal climate" and the number of English-speaking expats residing there – but these places, not far from Mexico's second largest city, also became headlines when Americans were found murdered there.

"They were in the wrong place at the wrong time," explained people quoted in the news stories. "They should have known better: You don't go out here alone at night … especially to certain places. You travel only on the major highways and roads. Don't wander around. You learn that, to stay safe, it's wise to live in a gated community."

That wasn't what we wanted; our dream included late-night strolls along cobble stone streets of old towns with lots of lanes and paths.

Mexico's Yucatán peninsula – home to cruise ships calling on expansive, intentionally constructed resort destinations like Cancún, Cozumel, and Playa del Carmen – advertised itself as Mexico's "safest place to be." Yet, rather than these tourist traps featuring all-inclusive vacations and panhandlers shilling free meals at luxurious spots in exchange for touring the premises and listening to pitches on the benefits of buying their time-shares, we decided to take a close look at the historic city of Mérida and its nearby beaches—especially Progreso.

It's hot there. Very hot. Hot and humid and buggy.

I like the heat—just not tropical rain forest heat. And I don't like bugs. But almost everything's air-conditioned and, once you become acclimated to the weather, it isn't so bad ... at least most of the time.

We stayed in a charming little hotel in downtown Mérida, on a small street not far from the city's market. With Walmart, Costco, Home Depot, Office Max, and other U.S. brands, we felt "at home," although stifled by the climate if not put off by the language.

But Mérida wasn't where we wanted to be—even its own people looked to escape the oppressive heat by heading to the beaches, not even an hour's drive away. We headed there, too.

Russ and I had traveled there to look at "Big Blue," a property in Progreso, just two blocks from the Gulf of Mexico beach. The stately building boasted five big bedrooms, five full baths, a separate "casita" with its own facilities, and a heart-shaped swimming pool ... all enclosed and private. We'd seen it listed online by more than one property agent based in Mérida, although one seemed to be more familiar with the property and the Canadian family that was selling it. It had been on the market for a while, the agent informed us, and the owners were "motivated" to sell it.

"What does that mean?" we asked.

"Come down and look at it," replied the agent. "I've spoken with the sellers and feel sure that they'll sell it to you for $10,000 less than their asking price."

That's why we flew down to Mérida and drove out to Progreso.

The house was truly awesome. But it needed work. And furnishings. Especially if it were to become the bed and breakfast we envisioned. How much would it cost us to have the repairs and updates made, with so many trades – electrical, masonry, plumbing, carpentry – involved? What would we pay for all the new appliances – air conditioners, a commercial kitchen, all the usual suspects – that needed upgrading? And what kind of estimate would be appropriate for the furnishings, especially comfortable new bedrooms and mattresses?

For three days, we divided our tasks. The property agent had a brother who, as a construction overseer, had contacts with all the local trades who'd come in and provide "reasonable estimates" for the work that needed to be done. Meanwhile, Russ and I would hit all the big box stores to get an idea of what the appliances and furnishings would run.

We made an offer—exactly what the agent told us the owners would accept. Leaving later that morning, we waited at the airport for a response, laptops opened and WiFi on. Just before boarding, we received the news: "Sorry. The owners changed their minds. They'll sell you the house … but want the full asking price."

Six years on the market. We offered what was recommended before we flew down to check out the property and Progreso. But, now, it didn't feel right. If we were misled about the acceptable price for the property, what else might be mistaken? Perhaps all those quotes from the property agent's brother weren't reliable, either?

A bit disappointed, but convinced we'd made the right decision in not pursuing this property, we headed back to Wisconsin.

Where should we consider next?

# # # # #

I engaged and employed all my contacts and connections in seeking a church that was seeking a pastor. Preferably a Spanish-speaking pastor. Like the patriarch Abraham long ago before me, I felt a tugging at my spirit urging me to move on to a place whose Spirit would call.

That's when I came across this mission statement from an international church in Panama serving all people, but especially English and Spanish speakers, which was looking for a new lead pastor:

"To be a bridge of cooperation and understanding

18

among religious groups of all faiths; of acceptance of others regardless of social class, race, gender, or sexual orientation; between all of God's children, mirroring and practicing the love God has for us; of freedom in the study of religion, the interpretation, and the practice of faith; and for God's love in a troubled world, expressing a generosity of spirit to all those in need."

Now, that sounded like a perfect fit in terms of my personal beliefs.

I submitted a letter of application, along with my CV, via email.

"Hi Reverend Bruce, thanks for contacting us!" I heard back, almost immediately. "We are thrilled to receive a note of interest from someone with your background and we would be glad to forward you the application package. We hope you find the opportunity interesting and hope to get to know you." With regards, the message was signed by the pastoral search committee chair.

# # # # #

Within days of completing and submitting the application materials requested, I heard back from the pastoral search committee: "We would like to schedule an interview this coming Monday. Any chance we can hold it at 7pm or 8pm CST?" It would be an hour conversation.

The plot was thickening, but what did we really know about living in Panama? Our only experience with the country was a cruise ship excursion through Panama City, culminating on a boat that would take us through the fabled Panama Canal. But what would it be like to live there? What was its quality of life and cost of living? Even closer to the equator than Jacksonville, Florida, or Progreso and Mérida, Mexico, how hot and humid would the climate be there?

We did a bunch of research online, as I awaited my phone interview. Theologically and ministerially, the interview went quite well. I was offered the job, which I was unprepared to either accept or reject. There were too many questions that needed answers.

Panama is very, very hot and very, very humid. It is also very expensive, especially the areas around the church. How much would it cost us to move there—including our three dogs? Would the church help defray some of these costs? When did they expect me to start? How long would it take for us to sell our house and our cars? Would the church pay for Russ to join me for a week or so to do house-hunting, while I was being oriented to the church?

Ultimately, there were more questions than answers forthcoming. And those answers that were provided indicated that the move would be more difficult than either Russ or I had anticipated.

Sadly, I turned down the offer. But I continue to use this church's mission statement as an example of what I believe a church should be.

# # # # #

We were beginning to become indoctrinated to the "expat" community and decided to consider the possibilities offered by two other countries in South and Central America: Ecuador and Nicaragua.

During a year in high school, Russ's family had hosted an exchange student from Ecuador. More recently, we were hearing increasingly good things about expat life in this country: Relatively low crime, a large and active expat community, extremely generous homes at very affordable prices, and quite a comfortable climate … even in Cuenca, a beautiful colonial city high up in the mountains, where many expats have settled.

In Ecuador, you can enjoy some of the lowest prices in Latin America on everything from groceries to real estate and domestic help. A couple could easily live a modest lifestyle on as little as U.S. $1,200 per month, including rent. With less money needed for housing and utilities, retirees have the flexibility to travel and pursue other dreams. Inexpensive transportation is readily available and makes getting around the rest of the country a breeze.

Ecuador also offers great benefits to its senior residents, with discounts as high as 50% on things like international airfare and entertainment.

Many expats who retire to Ecuador find themselves extremely pleased with the country's medical system, particularly with the quality of care they receive. Most doctors speak English, and many trained in the U.S. Hospitals are excellent and equipped with state-of-the-art technology. Best of all is the cost: Health care can run anywhere from half to one-tenth the cost for the same services in the U.S.

Yes, we'd certainly think about Ecuador.

But we also were being tickled by Nicaragua, especially Lake Granada, a freshwater lake and the largest in Central America. The lake drains to the Caribbean Sea via the San Juan River, making its lakeside city an Atlantic port, although Granada (as well as the entire lake) is closer to the Pacific Ocean geographically.

Other parts of Nicaragua can get disturbingly hot, but Granada and its lake are quite comfortable and its real estate is altogether reasonable.

"Life here [in Granada] has been good to us," posted one retiree from the USA who was active in one of the Nicaragua online expat groups we had joined. "What you really need to think about is what you will do when you get here. Successful expats reinvent their lives and do things that they have always wanted to do. We do some volunteer work, are active in our church, and pursue interests we didn't have time for in our former life. We also travel a great deal. Central America is a great place to see. The availability in stores is great, although imported food is expensive. We have found most of what we want. We go to Managua once a month for groceries and to have a fun time," reported this Granada expat. But another expat living in Nicaragua had these words of warning about

Granada:

"You can live here very well on whatever income you have. We live in a middle-class neighborhood for a fraction of what it would cost in the U.S. or Canada. Our neighborhood is very safe, our neighbors are friendly and watch out for us, but you must practice common sense. Most of the crime is opportunistic and, if you are walking home drunk and talking on your iPhone at midnight, expect to invite trouble. We also avoid heavy tourist areas like La Calzada, which are magnets for crime. Be just as careful of expats as Nicas. Don't trust anyone you meet in a bar. Get to know people before you get too friendly."

Good advice. For everyone, no matter where.

While we had heard through the grapevine that "Nica" was the next best place to invest – because China was planning to spend lots of money building a canal there that would beat Panama's – there was just something about Nicaragua that made us uneasy. Maybe it was its history. Or, perhaps, it was because of El Salvador, Honduras, and (to a degree) even Costa Rica, its current neighbors, whose citizens were among the "immigrants" fleeing their countries to live in the United States. Whatever the cause of our hesitancy, neither Nicaragua or Ecuador, nor Mexico and Panama, felt right for us to retire there.

None of these places had our names on their welcome mats.

World Travelers

We know people who take trips to fabulous places by air, sea, and land. Some of them have been almost everywhere the world wantons, seeking its seven wonders and exploring places far from the beaten track.

For them, it's one exciting trip after another, going to places most of us only imagine and dream about, courtesy of TV's travel channels and the worldwide web.

What wonderful opportunities to be strangers in strange lands, to get away – truly away – for the vacation of a lifetime (or two).

We, however, have chosen another path … towards destinations that many simply cannot fathom. While enjoying periodic cruises, shopping for stuff purchased impulsively on a tourist's whim, and seeing how other people live (albeit from an American perspective), we prefer to return – year after year – to the same places: a small Spanish village where we spend a month unwinding after nearly a year's worth of frustrations … and, more recently, a small town in Portugal where dealing with frustrations occupy much of our time.

Sometimes, if we can manage it, we have made more than one trip to these places … spending an additional ten days to two weeks there the same year.

These times of living off the proverbial grid have become critical to our health and central to our overall perspective.

I not only get to speak with the natives, I speak as the natives do … picking up new slang and jargon, along with fluency. Where and when I can't converse, I learn how to communicate.

For a month, we move around like the locals—either walking a lot or driving cars with clutches that require us (sometimes) to pull up the emergency brake when forced to stop and then start again in the middle of a steep hill, with traffic honking behind us. For a month, we learn to ingest different kinds of foods and "delicacies" (pig jowls,

23

snippets of bull tails, pizza made with unusual ingredients, linings of cow stomachs, etc.). And, for a month, we try not to eat three meals daily – breakfast, lunch, and dinner – at our "normal" times: morning, noon, and (very) early evening … but, instead, to consume smaller "tapas" portions in the mid-afternoon and evenings (although we still prefer to eat at around 7:00 PM, not 10:00 PM).

But the biggest difference, we'd found, between being travelers passing through and living as part-time residents is learning to accept that other people and cultures tend to do things differently than we do. Which is perfectly all right. It's what makes the world go around!

Take patience, for instance—something I am sorely lacking.

In Iberia, we may wait at the bank for an hour or more while those ahead of us receive truly "personalized service" from customer reps. We have an 11:30 appointment at the Notario (the ultimate "lawyer's lawyer" in many EU nations), only to be seen an hour later than scheduled because the Notario's attention has been diverted by other matters. We sit in our attorney's office for much longer than we'd planned because – like our insurance agent – he takes the time (as much as needed) to be interrupted by telephone calls, other people coming into the office "just to ask a question," and whatever business that our agents can conduct while we're sitting there with them.

We have come to understand that when contractors tell us they'll be here at 10:00 but don't show up until 11:30 – and then take a two-hour lunch – before returning and working until 19:00 or 20:00, it's not because they're lazy or taking advantage … it's because the hands of a clock don't control them. They move to the beat of different drummers.

Ultimately, it's good for us, this learning to live in another culture that's different from our norm, and that a "mañana mentality," once adjusted to and accommodating it, indeed can be healthy.

In 2018, we no longer took month-long "vacations" to

our town in Portugal and Spanish village. We stayed. We became residents, if not citizens, of international oases where we'd passed snippets of our lives. For lots of reasons – practical and political – we decided to make Portugal and Spain our home bases.

We have come to understand that we're no longer travelers or tourists, but rooted residents, part and parcel of places that welcome us to other homelands and extraordinary communities.

House Hunters International: Portugal

People often ask us to compare our feelings about Portugal with Spain, where we've had a vacation bolt for more than ten years. It's as if we're being asked to choose fealty to one place over the other. We can't.

In some ways, Portugal and Spain are very similar – especially in terms of the inherent goodness of their people and beauty of the land – yet, in others, these countries have unique characteristics and personalities.

We love them both!

Portugal welcomed us and facilitated residing there; Spain put up barriers and made the list of "quehaceres" to live there full-time daunting and deliberate.

It all looks so simple on HGTV—buying a house in another country.

Trust me: it isn't!

Sure, it's fun to see what's for sale elsewhere and explore international properties online and via the telly. But putting your "boots on the ground" and confirming that what you see represented in all those come-hither Internet snapshots is actually what you'll be getting can be a real eye-opener. The fun stops and the headaches begin once you make an offer ... and it's accepted.

Why? Take closing costs, for instance.

Apart from any deposit or down payment, in Spain the transaction can cost you about 20% above and beyond the purchase price to cover transfer taxes, lawyer and Notario charges, and an assortment of administrative fees. So, a relatively inexpensive property purchased for 50,000 euros would cost about another €8-10K to own it legally.

Still relatively inexpensive, all things considered.

Friends told us that "settlement" costs in Portugal are much lower ... and we've learned that, actually, they are!

Consider purchase and transfer taxes on a property. In Spain, one now pays 8% of the property's value (its selling price) in taxes. While Portugal has several taxes that can accompany a property's purchase, if you're married and the place is your first and primary residence in Portugal, you'll pay only 0.8% in taxes on the purchase.

That's ten times the savings (vs. Spain's), just in taxes!

And Portugal grants most newcomer residents the first three years of ownership tax-free. If you fill out the forms—correctly and on time.

The lower costs to purchase property is one benefit of buying Portugal. The friendly, simpatico, but saudade Portuguese people is another. The history, the magnificent topography, and the exquisite monuments, memorials, castles and cobble stone streets of intimate towns and villages are yet others. Not only is Portugal's cost of living lower than that in many other countries, but it's quality of life is high.

All told, Russ and I made several trips to look at and evaluate properties in Portugal. We stayed in cozy little hotels and inns, wandering through their towns and cities. We attended seminars for people contemplating a move to Portugal or already living there. We narrowed our choices and looked at houses in the Coimbra and Castelo Branco areas.

We found what we were looking for in Lousa – not to be confused with Lousã in Coimbra – a small village about 20 minutes outside the city of Castelo Branco, with cobble stone streets and a church whose bells chime as a heartbeat punctuating the daily rhythm of life there.

Because of its proximity to Spain, the privacy of its separate guest quarters with en suite, and the potential of opening some sort of eatery in the property's former café, we purchased a property shown to us by a property agent using the flashlight of his phone.

The next day, when we returned to "tour" the town, we met the owner: a lovely, little old lady who communicated with us in a polyglot of Portuguese, Spanish, and (especially) French.

Despite her honesty and forthcoming answers to our questions, we've learned some valuable lessons about buying property in Portugal. First and foremost, always have your property inspected and its condition evaluated by a qualified professional. If you've seen the place online first and gotten excited about it, remember, too, that pictures and descriptions supplied by property agents put the best foot forward.

So, get a second opinion.

Thanks to our lawyer, Liliana Solipa, who represented us through our power of attorney, we were assigned fiscal numbers (NIFs), the property was purchased and put in our names, a bank account opened, the water and electricity turned on again.

That's when we decided to take advantage of a special sale offered by the airlines and spend a November week in our "new" Portugal home.

With keys in hand and hand on the front door handle, we quickly discovered how much work the place really needed after having been vacant and closed up for more than five years.

Moving Daze

"Dear Lord, what we gotten ourselves into? What have we done? Can it be fixed? How much will it cost? Is there any way we can get out of this? What do we do now?" I shook and sobbed as we showed the property we had purchased in Portugal to American friends who had been our neighbors only months earlier in Sturgeon Bay, Wisconsin, and were now again our neighbors, albeit on a quinta in Alpedrinha.

"It's pretty rough and sure does need some work," our friends agreed.

This was the first time we actually were seeing our future residence in the light. We bought it based on the pictures posted by its property agent on the Internet … the agent showing us the property, room by room, with the help of the little light emanating from his mobile phone (the power had been shut off) … and because the sweet, widowed little old lady who owned the place told us about how the building's café at street level had been the most popular watering hole in town.

When we next returned from the USA to begin making the property our own, however, we were devastated by what we saw once our attorney accompanied us to EDP, the power company, and had the electricity turned back on—including the lights.

Mold and mildew were everywhere, along with cracks in the walls and chinks in other places. Chunks of ceramic tile and entire steps had gone missing on the staircases. Missing, too, were puzzle pieces of wooden herring bone floors that had rotted when water ebbed in from the balconies.

The roof had leaked so much at the top of the steps that the door between the inside and the terrace was literally eaten away at its bottom. Shag carpet glued to the floor in the guest quarters was wet with water that smelled rotten. Hot water gushed through a hole in one bathroom ceiling, while no hot water came out of a kitchen sink or the shower in our other bathroom. (Yet, for some strange reason, there was an electric outlet inside the shower!)

Doors didn't open or close, as they had warped and no longer fit their frames properly. Two large glass panes covered by a retractable metal blind that fronted the café's windows were broken, and the metal blind wouldn't retract any longer. Kitchen cabinets constructed of particle board that looked good in pictures were crumbling and detaching themselves from the walls. Some lights worked, others didn't, and an antiquated electrical outlet wouldn't accommodate the brand new vacuum cleaner we'd purchased. When we plugged it into another socket, it tripped the house's circuit breaker.

Insulation? LOL! Zilch. The house was built with cement and concrete, with nothing between the internal and exterior walls.

There was neither rhyme nor reason to how the electricity and plumbing had been connected ... even the professionals shrugged, joking that, "that's how Portuguese houses are constructed."

Most of all, the place smelled morbid from being vacant, unoccupied, closed up, and unattended to for five years, maybe longer.

What looked good on paper and a dimly-lit walk through turned out to be more like a dystopian disaster. We had budgeted approximately U.S. $10,000-$15,000 for repairs and upgrades, a few new pieces furniture, air conditioning units, and perhaps a newly fitted kitchen. But what now yawned ahead of us appeared to be a bottomless money pit.

We learned that we'd need to up our electrical power from 15 to 30 Amps – a simple, cost-free function performed by the power company – especially if we intended to have air conditioners installed (essential here, where summer temps are a blazing 107° F/42° C for months), so it would be necessary to rewire the entire house: the old 1 mm wiring had to be replaced with 2.5 mm gauge to carry the increased current.

Ka-ching! Add another €3,500 to the budget.

Portuguese agents often identify their properties as "New," "Used," "Habitable," or "Ruina." Ours was specified as used; but, at best, it was habitable … especially given our American standards. We like to shower, shave, and shampoo daily … and can't bear it when even our dogs need air conditioning to survive without labored breathing.

Thanks to the contacts and connections we'd made through the expat networks, our property would be renewed and resurrected to a higher standard.

"Is it worth it?" some might ask.

"Good question!" we'd reply.

Compared to the typical Portuguese structures we'd seen, its rooms were large and legion, and their layout would work well for us. Beyond the commercial potential of its street-side café, there's a large eat-in kitchen and family room separated from the café by a cute courtyard. An outside marble staircase leads upstairs, in addition to an interior one that goes to all three floors. Azulejo tiles adorn the walls throughout and, for the most part, are intact and in excellent condition. Over the lower level kitchen are completely private guest quarters comprising a large bedroom, built-in closets, and an en suite. An oversize living room with balcony – along with two smaller rooms, formerly bedrooms but now used as a den, library, and separate storage room – make up the second floor. Upstairs on the third is a large master bedroom featuring a big walk-in wardrobe, as well as an en suite. An adjacent "great" room has become our breakfast room, efficiency kitchen, home office, and bedroom for the three small dogs. All this plus a massive covered terrace with grilling area, electric washer and dryer, and plenty of space for tables, chairs, and lounges. New windows and doors are throughout.

To live in one of the world's most beautiful, peaceful, and welcoming countries brings its own rewards. But when one's quality of life is high compared to such a relatively low cost of living that we can live quite comfortably on my monthly Social Security payments – including comprehensive health care coverage for two, one 55 and the other almost 70 – there's no doubt whatsoever that we've achieved a remarkable return on our investment.

"But why Lousa?" people often ask. "Why live in such a tiny town with only a couple of cafés, one corner market, and not a single shop?"

Because the people were welcoming and the "fit" felt right.

Besides, we're their own crazy American guys – os loucos americanos – who walk their dogs on leashes and carry around plastic "poopy" bags to pick up after them, depositing the trash into street bin receptacles. Rumor had it, we learned later, that the locals thought we had wives stashed in the house who we never allowed outside!

We thrive on taking walks with our dogs along its narrow, cobble stone streets crossed by fractional lanes and paths, all bearing their special names and history on corner-side plaques affixed to the houses. And, perhaps, because there's a special sense of inter-connectivity between the quirky, lopsided properties small and large attached one to another and the people who pass us on the street jabbering away in a language that sounds like an unlikely cross between French and Hungarian.

And we're determined to learn it!

JAX & Company

"Come here for a second, Russ, you have to see this …"

En route from Racine, Wisconsin, to Jacksonville, Florida, where I had accepted the call to pastor an interdenominational church, we stopped to pick up some cat food for the kitty we'd rescued.

"What do you want to show me?" Russ asked, his hands holding catnip and toys for our three-day drive from the upper Midwest to the lower Southeast.

"Look!" I pointed at a small white puppy playing alone in a kennel crate, rolling over repeatedly and making the funniest faces.

"Cute," Russ contributed.

"Can we ask to see him in one of the cubicles and play with him a bit? The dog is a Miniature Schnauzer. Have you ever seen a white one?"

"But we've got a three-day drive ahead of us," Russ interjected. "Besides, it's a male."

We'd never had a male dog, always assuming females were friendlier, easier to train, more obedient and loyal.

(You know what's said about ass-u-me!)

Discretion being the lesser part of valor when it comes to canines in our lives, within 30 minutes the puppy had become the newest member of our family … accompanied by bags filled with food, toys, and treats.

The little boy and I bonded during our drive to the sunshine state, me driving and he lounging on the rented Chevy Tahoe's massive center console. Russ had the cat in his car, growling all the way.

We named our new family member Jackson – Jax for short – in respect to our Florida destination. It was there that he'd have his first bath, his first grooming, his first set of rabies and distemper shots, his first taste of a poison pill ("Comfortis") his sensitive system couldn't quite handle to combat the ferocious fleas and ubiquitous bugs – flying, crawling, hiding, biting – inhabiting the same space that we did.

Walking him around our block in the Springfield area where we lived, I would sometimes encounter a gentleman walking his two dogs: a tiny Yorkshire and a larger black one that looked like another terrier.

"Is that a Scottie?" I asked.

"No. She's a black Schnauzer."

"I've never seen a black Schnauzer …"

"And I've never met a white one!" he said.

Jackson is the smartest, most sensitive, and affectionate dog we'd ever adopted. Yes, males can be quite loving. Still, when the cat passed on, we decided to find Jax a female companion.

The chance of finding any Schnauzers in the classified ads of our local back-home-in-Virginia newspaper was next to nil. Yet, there was the ad: "Miniature Schnauzers. Home-raised. Parents on premises …"

"Should we call?" I asked Russ.

No answer was needed.

"Hi, I'm calling about your newspaper ad for Miniature Schnauzers," I began when the phone was answered. "We're looking for something very specific: a black female. I don't suppose you have one?"

"Actually, we do. Two pups are left: a black bitch and a salt-and-pepper male, the runt of the litter. Want to see them?"

"We'll be right there," I informed the pets' surrogate parents. Looking at Russ, I then matter-of-factly stated, "You know what this means."

The black girl was exactly what we'd hoped for; but the little silver and gray boy was totally unexpected: a bundle of joy that jumped into our laps, licked our throats, and rolled over for his belly to be rubbed. Russ shot me a look that clearly declared, "We're not leaving with one dog. Either both of them are coming home with us, or neither will."

That's how we came to have three dogs – the "children," as we refer to them – who totally have changed our lives.

34

If and when you decide to make a major move, to another country, across the great pond, in addition to your own visa requirements, you will need to ensure that all their paperwork is properly presented. With pets originating in the European Union, you get official pet passports that enable them to cross borders. For pets coming into the EU from the USA, you work with your veterinarian and the U.S. Department of Agriculture to complete comparable documents, reasonable facsimiles.

Before all this happens, however, you must deal with the airlines if you won't want your pets to be transported in the plane's cargo hold.

Physicians qualified our dogs as Emotional Support Animals to fly with us in the cabins of three American Airlines' flights—between Green Bay, Wisconsin, and Madrid, Spain. Upon landing in Madrid, authorities hardly glanced at all the details and data included on the eleven-page document. They simply scanned the spots where each of the dogs had a microchip inserted and confirmed their numbers matched the papers.

The person handling our rental car warned us that, in Spain and Portugal, dogs and cats must be "restrained" in vehicles, either by keeping them in their carriers or affixing them to the seat belt locks through a simple device where one side connects to their collars, the other to the seat belt buckles. Amazon sells a set for about ten dollars.

Somewhat comforted to find great vets who speak English, you make an appointment and bring your pets in for exams – "consultations" – where you spend over an hour together and more than €200 … which not only includes thorough exams, but eight-month collars to guard against fleas, ticks, and the dreaded Leishmaniasis, more medicine to combat it and yet more medicine to guard against heart worms.

"You must realize," the vet warns, "that dogs and cats from other countries (i.e., the USA) are more susceptible to disease, mosquito bites, and attacks." In a plastic bag are the medicines, dosages and schedules they're to be given, brochures, and other paraphernalia; you're handed directly three official pet passports (included in the fees), enabling your dogs or cats to travel between EU countries.

In exchange, you hand over your Multibanco card and cringe when the ticket prints out a receipt for two hundred and eight euros, equal to about U.S. $242.00. Then you remember how much time the vet has spent with you and your three pooches; all the medications, pills, and elixirs you've received to take home; the three, 3-in-1 combination vaccines protecting your cherished ones against Bordetella bacteria, Canine Parainfluenza virus, and Adenovirus Type 2. How much would all that have cost you in the USA? Undoubtedly, a heck of a lot more!

And when the vet hands you the itemized "factura" (invoice), you learn that professional health care for your pets is tax-deductible in Portugal.

Pet passports in hand, you and your pets now need licenses from your local junta. "You will want to have them," your veterinarian advises. "Without licenses, the police can come and take away your pets if people make complaints."

Each of our dogs gets a license. Just €10 for the first year—for all three. We leave with the distinguished documents, words offset by seals and stamps and signed by the junta's president.

Just when we think there won't be anything else the dogs need, the devil pays a house call: one, then the others, fall sick. We grieve their pain, discomfort, and suffering, even as we curse the ceaseless messes everywhere. So, we make another appointment with the vet.

This time we bring just Jax, as he's the only one sick at the moment. Again, we're impressed by the thoroughness of care and concern shown by our dog's doctors: a physical exam ... x-rays to ensure there's no "foreign" matter in his intestines (or other internal parts) ... nearly an hour's worth of IV solution to replenish the liquids lost during his "accidents" and absence of appetite ... antibiotics by injection ... pills, antibiotics plus probiotics to help him heal at home … advice to boil a skinless breast of chicken and some rice, feeding him in small doses.

The veterinarian hands us two little bags of pills and her card with the practice's 24-hour emergency line, then jots down her own personal phone number on it, too. "If Jax isn't improving in 24 hours – or if he has any more problems – call and bring him back tomorrow," she said.

Ninety-four euros. The bill for all that attention!

Jax began to improve almost immediately. But the two littles ones quickly came down with the same symptoms. We concluded the problem was food poisoning, not from something they'd picked up in the streets from well-meaning people who'd leave bones and gristle for the town's homeless animals. No, the problem was with their food.

We'd purchased the best food available – dry and canned – in an area shop similar to Fleet & Farm, since everything in the supermarkets has cereal as a primary ingredient and far too much fat for dogs who suffer from pancreatitis.

Forcing them to swallow their pills, followed by feeding them the boiled chicken and rice, all three quickly regained their health. Portuguese friends recommended a new pet supply shop that had just opened, where we purchased excellent low-fat and grain-free dry food: just two small bags (2-3 kgs), along with four cans of low-fat, "all-natural" food without any additives—turkey with raspberry, chicken with pineapple, chicken with apple, and chicken fillets.

With a new customer discount, our bill totaled €33— almost U.S. $40.

Whether standard, off-the-shelf supermarket brands heavy with fillers, or highly nutritious specialty foods found only in limited locations, pet foods are among those daily breads (or breeds) that can cost more here in Spain and Portugal than in the USA.

Even so, the money is well spent on health care for our furry families.

Three Dog Nights

Forgive me: I've gotten ahead of myself – and you – in our narrative. So, please, let me digress:

"If they can't come with us, we're not going," my partner and I agreed. If our three Miniature Schnauzers – our children, now that our biological one was grown – couldn't travel with us and be allowed entry into the EU, we wouldn't follow our hearts and minds to Portugal and Spain ... much as we were distraught and disillusioned with what has been happening in the United States.

That meant not only would we expect our dogs to fly in the cabin with us – not the cargo hold – for all three flights from Green Bay, Wisconsin, to Madrid, Spain ... but it also presumed that they would be allowed to pass through Immigration in Spain and then into Portugal without any beastly requirements.

Bringing our furry family members with us would become the most complex and frustrating part of making a new home on the other side of the big pond.

The "kids," as we refer to them, had lived with us in Florida, Wisconsin, and Virginia. But whenever we traveled to our vacation bolt in southern Spain, we'd leave them at home with carefully vetted pet-sitters.

Now, our future depended on them being there with us.

Fortunately, due to our own personal maladies, the dogs were qualified as "service" animals with the airlines. Unfortunately, there are three of them and only two of us.

American Airlines was the only carrier that would allow two people to bring three designated service dogs aboard ... and that was only after (working with our travel agent) we completed their forms, had medical testimonies vouchsafed by our doctors and submitted to the airlines, and were interrogated in telephone interviews by airline officials.

We qualified and our dogs were approved to travel with us!

But that just covered their transportation. Getting them

into the European Union was another matter that would require entirely different documents and protocols.

They're called "pet passports" in the EU. But they're issued only once you're inside the EU. Emigrating from the United States, one needs to complete a reasonable facsimile – an official EU Health Certificate – specific to the language and place of entry. For us, that was Spanish, as our entry to the EU would be through Madrid's Barajas airport.

The eight-page bilingual document, requiring a separate 22-page set of instructions for completing it, attests that each of the named and described dogs has received a state-of-the-art microchip (manufacturer's name and number identified), followed by a new rabies shot (with batch number and effective dates identified). It had to be filled out by a USDA-accredited veterinarian and then certified by the appropriate United States Department of Agriculture office in our state.

Was our vet USDA-accredited?

"Darned if I know," Dr. Randy laughed. "I'm certified by the American Veterinary Association and by the Wisconsin Veterinary Association. Does that count?"

Nope. He had to be USDA-accredited.

Try finding the USDA office in your state specifically charged with handling documentation for pets traveling abroad. It took us two weeks through a variety of sources and referrals to find that USDA office in Madison, Wisconsin.

The amiable USDA rep who helped us deal with the process confirmed that Dr. Randy was, in fact, USDA-accredited and advised us to have him inject the microchips and rabies shots between three and four weeks before we traveled, and to go back and have him sign all the paperwork ten days before leaving. We were then to send the docs via overnight mail from our city to the USDA's office in Madison ($50) and to enclose a postage-paid return overnight envelope (another $50) so that, theoretically, we'd have them in hand a week before our travel. Apart from the vet costs, we'd need to pay the USDA's $38 certification fee.

Signed, sealed, and delivered!

Our dogs were ready to enter the European Union, traveling with us as passengers aboard our American Airlines flights.

Instead, Mother Nature intervened.

Philadelphia – where our flights from Chicago and to Madrid connected – was hit by a severe snowstorm. Even before the airport officially closed, we received email notifications that our flights from Chicago to Philadelphia and Philadelphia to Madrid had been cancelled.

Our choices were few and far between. The best American Airlines could do was to put us on the "same" flights … only five days later! In the meantime, we'd have to stay put at the airport motel (since we already had sold our house, our cars, our furniture, as we planned to stay in Portugal).

I called our travel insurance hotline. Fortunately, we were told, everything – the extra days at the motel, meals, transportation, even clothing and cosmetics – would be covered, except for the extra dog food. Yeah, uh-huh. (But that's another story entirely, for later.)

That night, I awoke with a subconscious jolt: What about the dogs, I wondered? With the tight timeline for arrival in the European Union, their paperwork would expire three days before our rescheduled flights arrived. Surely, it couldn't be that big of a deal? Surely, the immigration officials would understand that our flights were delayed because a blizzard had hit Philadelphia. Surely, they would wave us through, as we only exceeded the deadline by three days? Surely, there wouldn't be any real problems?

I wasn't so sure …

So, I called my friendly USDA representative in Madison, Wisconsin, from our motel next to the Green Bay airport. After explaining the situation, he warned me, "You will need to get them new papers. The European

Union won't care one iota about cancelled flights or any explanation you give. As far as they're concerned, you've passed their deadline; your paperwork is null and void."

Best case scenario if we used our existing documentation our three dogs would probably be quarantined somewhere in Madrid for three weeks (or more). Worst case scenario? We'd be turned away and sent back to the USA ... without the dogs designated as service animals, they'd be flying in the baggage hold on whatever flights could be arranged.

Discretion being the better part of valor, we decided to obtain the new paperwork. We downloaded and completed the forms as fully as possible, based on the current documents we had in hand. A friend drove in from our former hometown an hour away and loaned us her van. We raced back to the vet's office in Sturgeon Bay with the dogs and our new paperwork ... had him sign the papers ... took the papers to our local pack-and-ship store, paying another $50 to overnight the papers to the USDA in Madison and $50 for a reply envelope to us c/o our airport motel ... and $38 for the USDA's updated certification.

Fortunately, the paperwork arrived like clockwork.

The flights, however, were another matter.

Our American Eagle flight from Green Bay to Chicago was operated by an American Airlines affiliate, with its rules for the dogs: The biggest one must remain in his carrier, seated on our laps. From Chicago to Philadelphia, we flew on American Airlines itself, which took our big boy's carrier and placed it in the baggage hold, telling us the dog could sit on our laps ... but not in a carrier. The longest leg of our trip – from Philadelphia to Madrid – had a United Airlines crew (United had just merged with American, but neither were on the same page yet in terms of their procedures.) We waited about 15 minutes while the flight attendants discussed how to handle us and our dogs. Finally, we all agreed to sit in the absolute last row of seats in the cabin – three seats in the middle, with Russ at one aisle and me on the other, an empty seat for the dog between us. The dog was a great passenger who seemed to enjoy flying, as well as all the attention from other passengers.

We arrived early the next morning in Madrid, not knowing who – or where – we'd be asked to show the dogs' docs. Not the customs agent who stamped our passports. Nor the immigration agent whose station we needed to pass through after retrieving our luggage.

Just as we were about to leave the airport building for the rental car area, a man dashed out of an adjoining vestibule. "The paperwork, please, for the dogs," he asked in Spanish. We handed over our new, eight pages of documentation.

He looked only at one page, bypassing every sheet of paper with the dates and signatures and certifications. Of interest to him only were the microchips, which he waved over each dog with a wand to confirm that the numbers listed on our papers agreed with the numbers shown on the wand.

They did.

It was a long, complicated, and exacting trip that lasted some 18 hours with our dogs.

Would we do it all over again if the need be?

You bet we would!

How can you begin a new life in another country without your "family" … even if they've got four legs and fur?

I don't know about you, but we certainly can't.

Learning the Lingo

Obrigado.

"Thank you."

In three short trips between Spain and Portugal before moving lock, stock, and barrel to Portugal, that's about the sum total of the vocabulary we've learned ... except, of course, for "Bom dia!"

The Portuguese tend to be a very friendly and courteous people.

As Russ and I are coming to grips with the property we purchased in Portugal and everything it entails — electric company, water company, tax office, government offices, window and door contractors, electricians, plumbers, et al — a Spanish friend leaned in and bent my ear a bit:

"Just remember to fill up your car's tank with gas at the last petrol station you come to whenever entering Portugal," he advised. "And, while you're filling up, don't forget to purchase your card for any toll road highways you'll be traveling on."

Good advice.

On average, gasoline (petrol) costs @ 10-20 cents more per liter in Portugal than in Spain. And unlike USA toll roads where you have the option of either stopping, queuing up, and paying the attendant in cash or prepaying your trips by credit card and posting a decal read by the toll trolls that debit each rite of passage from your account, it doesn't work like here.

BEFORE embarking on a Portuguese toll road, one must have the appropriate documentation purchased, verified, and posted on his or her vehicle. Hence, my friend's suggestion about buying the decal at the last gas station we encountered in Spain before entering Portugal. The problem, however, was two-fold: (1) Unlike most civilized countries – including many places in Portugal – which distinguish between gasoline and diesel fuels, our (diesel) tank was close to empty as we entered three separate fueling stations. All offered various grades of gasoline; (2) none, however, appeared to carry diesel fuel … until we learned that in some places, diesel fuel is referred to as "gasoleo."

With my limited Spanish attuned to the Portuguese attendant's even more restricted familiarity with the Spanish language, I ultimately realized – after showing him a credit card and repeating "carretera" (highway) several times – he was telling me that toll road decals are sold at the post office two roundabouts down the road, on the left-hand side of the street.

Highway decals aren't the only things sold at post offices in Portugal. That's where you post your mail, can pay your utility bills, and complete certain government forms. So, it took nearly an hour for our turn with the facility's sole post mistress.

Fortunately, she spoke a token English and understood the transaction we were seeking to complete. We could buy decals good for 5 to 40 euros worth of toll road, but needed to pay cash, since our American credit and debit cards didn't work there. Then, we needed to scratch off the coating to find the secret letters and numbers encoded beneath.

Next, we were to text the number printed in tiny 4-point type on the card and provide our secret code, PIN number, and "matrícula" – the rental vehicle's license plate number and country where registered – using our mobile phone. In return, we would receive a special "SIM" which we were to write on the ticket and place it on the car's windshield.

Except that I can't text. And neither of us had access to a cell phone that functioned in the European Union.

Assured (we believed) that we had 48 hours before additional fees and fines would be posted to our rental car bill, we decided to take a chance and get on the toll road … without completing all the required rigmarole. After already spending seven hours for what Google promised would be a five-hour journey, we were exhausted with all the mistakes that its Maps and Directions functions put us through and hoped that the desk clerk at our hotel would be kind enough to call and fix the problem for us.

She did, God bless her!

Not having eaten since early in the morning, we decided we had earned ourselves a good meal at a restaurant not too far from the hotel. Russ and I both were in the mood for Asian food – Thai, Chinese, Japanese, whatever – and were delighted to discover such an eatery just around the corner.

Ever see those Asian restaurant menus where meals don't have names, just pictures and numbers? That's where we ate. Whatever our earlier challenges in trying to communicate between Spanish and Portuguese, we now encountered a more complicated challenge: Our hostess spoke no English or Spanish ... just Portuguese and Chinese.

"No limits," she explained, pointing to the words printed on the menu in English. After about ten minutes, we finally understood that this was an "all you can eat" restaurant. But, rather than the groaning board buffets we were used to, we were to pick out one item at a time, which would be brought to our table in a small side dish. Chopsticks, not cutlery, and napkins were provided. Actually, the food was rather good for a Chinese restaurant in Castelo Branco, Portugal. By the time we were up to our third choice, however, we could sense that even at a restaurant with "no limits," enough was enough, according to management.

Now settling into our home, our little town, and the "big city" 15 minutes down the road and round the roundabouts, we're excited about how far we've come.

Tonight, we begin our official Portuguese language class.

You're Welcome, Portugal!

It's a different world.

And another time.

A place where the land still is vibrant and verdant and determines not only how people work, earn their livelihoods, and put food on their tables ... but the very stuff of life itself.

A time where people still "hang out" in the street sharing small talk with family and friends; watching their youngsters ride scooters or sit on their stoops, playing make-believe games together. People are walking — to the grocery, the café around the corner, or just moving aside so that an errant automobile can pass along the narrow roadways. In doorways, you can see the shadows of others, more elderly, waving at the passing parade.

It's hard to believe that today is Monday, a week since we've arrived in Lousa-Escalos de Cima, Castelo Branco, Portugal. We are captured and caught up in the little things that rinse and spin the fabric of our life.

Even more amazing is that our daily routines — our home, what and where we're eating, how our friends and family in the next towns over are doing and feeling — have changed so dramatically since we moved here.

Facebook no longer is the be-all-and-end-all; it's simply a convenience: a more practical and efficient way to stay in touch. A quick skim of the postings shows that almost nothing has changed back in the USA: The atrocities, indignities, wrongdoings being committed by those at the pinnacles of power continue unabated, even as those seeking justice and decency continue to clamor.

Forgive me for not spending my usual hours poring over each new revelation and agonizing over every horror happening on the other side of the pond. See, except for a bizarre new curse word uttered with ironic derision, "Trump & Company" doesn't live here.

Without all that cacophony and static, I'm much calmer—happier and more joyful. I'm too caught up here and now in the dazzling blue skies, the birds chirping special songs, the shuffling of feet and echo of voices passing our way.

There's a certain sweet melancholy ("saudade") to the Portuguese people that draws you in and keeps you enchanted. It's as if you're among family, beyond a circle of special friends.

Portugal welcomed us and facilitated residing there; Spain put up barriers and made the list of "quehaceres" to live there full-time daunting and deliberate.

People often ask us to compare our feelings about Portugal with Spain, where we've had a vacation bolt for more than ten years. It's as if we're being asked to choose fealty to one place over the other. We can't.

In some ways, Portugal and Spain are very similar — especially in terms of the inherent decency of their people — yet, in other ways, the two countries have unique character and personalities.

We love them both!

Taking Stock (and Stocking Up)

Today marks two months (plus a day or so) since we left the USA to begin a new life as expats in Portugal. Honestly, it hasn't been easy. There have been expected challenges and unanticipated ones … the latter often costing more in frustration and finances than the former.

Since landing at Madrid's Barajas airport, we rented a car and drove to Lousa, our little village in Portugal, with three miniature schnauzers, three large pieces of luggage, and two carry-on computer cases stuffed with passports, visa documents, and all those really important papers hitherto stored in a bank's safe deposit box.

Almost immediately upon arrival in Portugal, we signed a two-year contract with MEO to provide high-speed Internet, television, and telecommunications services.

We purchased a car – giving up our former Mercedes, BMWs, Audis, Jaguars, and Jeeps for a more practical Ford – along with a "Via Verde" windshield gadget, and managed to register it to deduct tolls directly from our Portuguese bank account. We've been to the bank (too many times), learning how to conduct many if not all financial transactions through "Multibanco" ATM machines. And we visited the tax office, Finanças, where we paid the vehicle's "road tax." Later, we returned to Finanças to pay last year's property tax and request a future exemption according to Portuguese property law.

Our dogs have been to the veterinarian, where they were examined and vaccinated for everything under the Iberian sun … and took home eight-month collars and medicine to protect them against fleas, ticks, and the dreaded leishmaniasis (as well as heartworms). While at the vet's office, we also obtained official European Union pet passports for all three. (Our bill came to €200, considerably more than the nine euros we paid for both Russ and me to see a doctor and get our prescriptions refilled. But, here in Portugal, vet bills are legitimate income tax deductions!) Pet passports in hand, we visited our local "junta's" freguesia (town office), where we filled out more paperwork and paid an additional nine euros for three initial annual dog licenses.

Speaking of the freguesia, we got to know Bruno, its administrator, who helped us with expediting and certifying mail – he also serves as our town's local postmaster – but, more importantly, in obtaining the official "Atestados de Residencia" that would be essential not only in having our container of household goods from the USA released from the port of Lisbon and delivered to our home here, but also serve as an additional vital document to be considered during our appointment at SEF (Serviço de Estrageiros e Fronteiras), where – prayerfully – our four-month residency visa would become a one-year residency card.

It did.

After two hours of paper-shuffling and copying, fingerprinting, and digital photos taken, our residency was approved. We were handed papers documenting that fact, and told that our official residency cards would arrive approximately two weeks later. Delivered by courier, the cards arrived two weeks later—to the day! Good thing we were here – at home – because our signatures were required.

We took a ten-day "vacation" to Spain, where we did our best to remedy the damages suffered by our vacation place in Pruna, and then listed it for sale with the local property agents. After looking around at what we could afford that was available for sale in our preferred town of Olvera, we made a deal with the British gent who bought our original house there to buy it back from him – lock, stock, and barrel – at a very substantial discount.

# # # # #

Returning to Portugal, we unpacked and cleaned the dust and damp that had settled throughout our house after being vacant and closed up for nearly six years. We had chunks of walls with mildew and ceilings covered with mold removed, replaced with fresh concrete and cement. Every surface was then painted with fresh licks of paint. We visited EDP, Portugal's energy service provider, and had our home's electric power upgraded from 15 to 30 Amps—and then hired an electrician to rewire the property and accommodate its increased current.

Oh, but there was lots more to do – still is! – inside our property.

The tiny downstairs kitchen had been patched together from out-of-the-box "wood composite" (sawdust!) cabinets assembled with Allen wrenches and plastic widgets. Cupboards above these cabinets were falling off the wall, affixed only by a couple of nails. Wedged into a corner, the sink was nearly impossible to get to or use; the refrigerator was rusty, smelly, and corroded inside. The large gas cooker and oven took up way too much space and was sticky with grime and grease.

We began by buying cleaning products. Lots and lots of cleaning products. First at the ubiquitous Chinese "markets" located on nearly every major street here in Castelo Branco. Then, at electrodoméstico (appliance) shops, as well as the "big box" stores, second-hand shops, and shopping centers (malls) located in the city's industrial zone. It was there that we found our kitchen cabinet maker. An entirely new kitchen with floor-to-ceiling cabinets, a functional sink, and matching granite counters and backsplashes against our irregular 75-degree angled walls would soon be ours, joining a new refrigerator, vitroceramic top electric cooker and oven, and used kitchen table and chairs from Holland.

Simultaneously, we replaced old and broken wooden double-doors, a casement window, and the hollow door at the top of the steps whose ragged, jagged bottom had been eaten away by poor drainage and leaks with new aluminum products. We splurged to the tune of about €200 to have "mosquiteras" (screens) added to most of our windows and doors to deter the mosquitoes, gnats, and – especially – big, black flies from taking our home hostage.

Yes, we shopped until we've dropped! We've been to our local and regional health centers, where we paid to register and confer with a doctor. We purchased prescriptions at pharmacies, food at groceries and supermarkets, furniture and appliances at local shops and big box stores. We got gasóleo at petrol stations and canisters ("bottles") of propano at our corner market. We've been to AKI and Brico Marché, repeatedly, for household goods and supplies. At Monday's Fundão market, we bought plants, bric-a-brac and clothing. We even went to an "estate sale" or two, where we negotiated the prices of a few antiques, collectibles, and assorted non-essentials.

All this, attempted and accomplished by us with sales people and associates who speak Portuguese, but very little English. We were doing our best to learn Portuguese, having attended the first five official classes offered in our area. We shopped and read labels, studied store circulars and promotional materials while seated on the throne in our bathroom, and menus at all the places we've eaten while we've been without a kitchen. We joined Portugal-based groups on Facebook and looked to purchase used and second-hand goods on OLX. Using our few poorly pronounced words in Portuguese bolstered by body language and a smattering of Spanish, we made ourselves understood. And, despite the misunderstandings that occasionally occurred, Portuguese-only speakers understood us more often than not.

We were communicating, if not conversing, with each other!

Thankful for all the support, advice, and encouragement we received through Facebook groups, we were fortunate to become acquainted and even friends with a bunch of really special people.

Best of all, we've been preoccupied—in good ways!

Except for our time following political posts on

Facebook, we learned to bypass and ignore the heinous acts and attitudes of Trumpism.

We no longer were fascinated but frustrated, focusing on every new tirade or travesty this illegitimate president and his circus of monkeys provoked. Instead, we enjoyed more peaceful pursuits, walking with our dogs along the meandering cobble stone streets of our little Portuguese village ... greeting neighbors with a "Bom dia" or "Boa tarde" ... and increasing our vocabulary to ask, "Como está?"

... Tá ben!

Ship(ment) of Fools

Thinking about shipping your household goods from the USA to Portugal, Spain, or anywhere else in the European Union?

Think again. And again. Very, very carefully!

From finances to frustrations, the entire process of getting your stuff from there to here (or here to there) can take a toll on even the most patient and persevering people.

(I'm persistent, yes! But patient? Hardly.)

Some international shipping companies are thieves, cheaters, and liars. I'd call how they operate and charge "highway robberies," but they're on the seas, not on land. So, let's just say I think they are pirates.

For argument's sake, start by trying to get a price quote on shipping your household goods – clothing, furniture, linens, artwork, tools, etc. – from various international shipping companies.

Go to Google. Enter "International-shipping-household-goods-USA-to-Portugal" (or wherever). Voilà! Up pops a list beginning with paid advertisers that supposedly are in the business of shipping your domestic drayage anywhere around the world. Most of the ad listings, especially, include "click-me" bait, offering free price quotes and/or estimates by filling out their online questionnaires on the specifications of your shipment. Your information is then shared with a number of shipping companies that will contact you, offering the "best deal anywhere," if you'll only complete their own set of questions, too.

Avid art lovers and collectors, all we really had wanted to ship from the USA to Portugal were about two dozen pieces of artwork that we treasured, because we'd found them in our 25 years of life together. Everything else we could leave behind: Adios, clothing. Adieu, furniture. Sayonara, dishes and glassware. Arrivederci, rugs and rags.

But, time and again, we were told by these international

moving companies that it's "more practical ... much cheaper, too," to ship a full container (a contrivance that measures approximately 8' x 8' x 20') than to share one with someone else or to ship – regardless of the transport means – a dozen or so boxes containing whatever.

So, we filled out the forms identifying what we would be shipping, including how many boxes and cartons of various sizes.

Responses ranged from the ridiculous to the sublime.

One highly-regarded and recommended company proposed an "all-inclusive" charge that brought its fee to more than twice what the others wanted ... but they shared an invaluable nugget of wisdom: Whichever company we ultimately chose to carry the contents of our lives across the Atlantic, be sure that (1) it included destination terminal handling charges and port charges, which many don't include or even mention; and (2) it is a member in good standing of FIDI, the largest global alliance of professional moving and relocation companies.

Based on our online communications, we narrowed our choice of international shipping companies to three. Only one belonged to FIDI. All were members of other moving industry alliances. We researched everything we could find that had been reported in reviews about each – positive and negative – and paid particular attention to their ratings and how they responded to complaints posted with the Better Business Bureau. We asked lots of questions, expressed our concerns, and requested clarifications.

Ultimately, we chose an international shipping company based on its price, communications, and reputation. Even before signing the contract and paying a deposit, we understood that the company was, essentially, our "broker" and liaison with other companies ... kind of like the hub of a wheel with many spokes: the company that came to our house to pick up everything we were shipping and deliver it to the port of Chicago; the company in the port of Chicago that unloaded the truck, packed it into a container, and put it aboard the ship; the actual "ship"ping company that would transfer our goods from one of its ships to another (and another), before arriving here in Portugal; the logistics company in Lisbon that handled all the paperwork and clearance procedures with Customs; and the company that would ultimately unload our container and deliver its contents to our home in Lousa.

Before anything at all can be imported "duty-free" to Portugal, however, one first must be granted a residence visa from a Portuguese consulate. Suffice it to say that household goods and personal effects can be imported duty-free by people establishing residency in Portugal who have secured a residency visa ... provided that these "household goods" were part of your previous residence and you don't have a furnished home in Portugal.

To qualify for this duty-free status, the goods must be accompanied by a "Baggage Certificate" (Certificado de Bagagem) issued by the Consulate handling your visa. The goods must be cleared through Customs within 90 days of their arrival in the country.

Obtaining the certificate isn't that difficult: You submit a list in triplicate of all items that you're sending to Portugal. Each numbered page should state, "List of Personal Effects of (Name)"; it can identify items by box (Box #1: Clothing, Box #2: Kitchen Utensils, Box #3: Books, etc.) or by description (King Size Bed and Mattress, Chest of Drawers, Artwork, etc.); and all electronic appliances must clearly list their serial numbers. The Consulate wants you to leave a few blank spaces after the last listing on each page for official signatures, and this statement must accompany your list: "I hereby certify that the above items have been in my use and possession for over six months" (Signature and date). Finally, a company, bank, or certified check – or a money order – payable to the Consular Section-Embassy of Portugal must be included and a postage paid, self-addressed (preferably trackable) envelope enclosed.

With all required documents in hand, scanned and sent

to the shipping company, we began packing and making certain that every box, along with every non-boxed item, was clearly numbered and identified exactly as listed on our official baggage certificate. Measuring off an area slightly less than 8 x 8 x 20 feet in our garage, we made sure that we didn't go beyond what would fit in the container.

Recalling the fires that had left so many Portuguese homeless and destitute not far from where we'd be living, we bought blankets, comforters, quilts, spreads, linens, towels, and curtains that could be used to wrap our household goods and then donated to those in need.

Unfortunately, the shipping company had other ideas.

The company insisted that, for insurance reasons, they needed to pack and "shrink-wrap" all of the furniture that we had so carefully covered with layers of blankets held tight to their contents with bungee cords. The unused blankets and coverlets would be shipped in other boxes.

Honestly, we experienced no real problems until about three weeks before our container was scheduled to arrive in Lisbon. The Portuguese "partner" of our American agent then requested additional documents.

Because our "contribuinte" – or fiscal – numbers had been obtained for us by our Portuguese attorney when we assigned her power of attorney to purchase our house, the forms showed her address. Not acceptable. To release our container from the port and deliver its contents to our home in Lousa, our address – not hers – was required. We contacted Liliana, our lawyer. Though it was no simple matter to have our address changed on the official documents, she was able to accomplish it for us. The new documents were forwarded to our Portuguese shipping agent.

"Perfect!" they exclaimed. "Now you must send us an official copy of your Atestado de Residencia," the document issued with a seal by the town hall of our jurisdiction and signed by its president. The Atestado declares that we are known to be living in the town. With a note hastily translated by Google and printed out, we rushed off to our local town hall (freguesia), where the document was produced for a small fee. Since the freguesia shared space with the local post office, the document was dispatched via DHL with guaranteed next-day delivery.

It got there just fine, but the document wasn't …

"No," argued the customer service agent at our shipping company. "The Atestados must state that you have been living in Lousa since the 25th of March."

But that wasn't true. I tried to explain that we had arrived on the evening of the 26th, due to delays in our flights. Then, each time we attempted to visit the town hall, it was closed. After all, it was the week before Easter and everything (along with everyone) was operating on limited schedules and hours. Very limited. It was April 3rd that we were finally able to get our Atestados de Residencia.

"No matter," she replied. "It is not our choice. Portuguese law requires that the documents be worded and dated precisely as I have stated." Well, fiddle-dee-dee. Now what? A newcomer to town, was I supposed to annoy the town hall clerk by trying to explain what was wrong, why and how it needed to be revised? "Never mind," the agent advised. "We will take care of it for you."

And they did. Somehow, they contacted the town hall's clerk in our tiny village and convince him not only to revise the document, affix the official seal, get the president to sign it again, and send it via courier to the shipping company's offices in Lisbon … without involving me or even an additional fee.

With all our papers and documentation in order, we waited for our shipment to arrive. Three times, we were notified that our ship would be delayed. Finally, it arrived: ten days later than anticipated. All things considered, not too bad.

But then came the bills from our Portuguese shipping representatives: €420 in port charges, to be paid immediately. I dashed out to the bank and transferred the funds. Immediately, came this reply: Your balance remaining is €970,00 … another €420 in "terminal handling charges" (THC) plus €550 for shuttle van service, as our street is too narrow for a truck to park and unload a 20 x 8 x 8 container. We knew we'd have no choice but to pay for this shuttle: we couldn't block the two-way traffic coming and going on the "main" street in town!

"Why did you wait to send me this second invoice?" I asked. "I just came back from driving to the bank to transfer the funds from your first payment request. Now, I have to go back again to transfer more money!"

Her explanation didn't make any sense whatsoever to me but, at that point, I didn't care anymore. It was only more money hemorrhaging. As long as the contents of our container were delivered on Wednesday …

They were.

But a bunch of stuff that we didn't pack, the movers did – an antique chest-of-drawers, a large baking "stone," some collectible glassware – arrived broken beyond repair. I sent emails and pictures of the damaged goods to everyone professionally involved with our move, but I still haven't heard a word back in reply. It's been over a week now.

As I said at the beginning of this chapter, if you are considering shipping household goods internationally, please think very carefully about it. Then, think again. And again.

Consider your options.

Our Health Care Providers

We went to see the doctor for the first time since arriving in Portugal.

No, nothing was wrong; our health, thankfully, is fine. But we had just about exhausted our medicines and needed to renew and refill our prescriptions. Which meant a visit to the doctor.

Consulting friends and acquaintances associated with us through the local online expat groups, a variety of suggestions and referrals were offered. Basically, they came down to these two:

(1) Find an English-speaking "private" doctor, pay for his/her time and services ("quite reasonable," we were told), and leave with the needed prescriptions to take to our local farmacia; or

(2) Begin using the Portuguese health system by visiting our town's "Centro de Saúde," where our primary physician would ultimately be located, and explain that we would pay directly for the services we needed now.

Of course, everything would rely on Google Translate, since the number of Portuguese words we knew – and could pronounce – only had expanded from five to about ten. Plus, we are Americans who, unlike our EU brethren that arrive in another Schengen nation with health cards and coverage from their homelands, we only had emergency medical coverage through our travel insurance. And, although we had been here for a month already with residency visas affixed to our passports, it would be another 20 days until our SEF appointment, when (hopefully!) our residency visa and required paperwork would provide us with proper residence permits—at least for a year, to begin with. This "real" residency, in turn, would enable us to register for the Social Security system and receive the necessary number (o número utente) to avail ourselves of the low-cost Portuguese health care system … even if we were to pay out of pocket or be covered by our health care insurance.

We decided to take our chances, first, and visit our little town's health center. Armed with a print out of the Google-translated document explaining (in Portuguese) who we are and why we were there, along with our NIF documents, passports and visas, medical records, and empty prescription pill bottles, I ventured a try during a day and time the sign posted on its door said the health center would be open.

Only a nurse was there that day. Using her best ten words of English interspersed with Portuguese, which I responded to with my only ten words of Portuguese interspersed with Spanish, I understood that she was telling me to come back the following Tuesday, any time after 10:00 AM, when the doctor would be there.

Unfortunately, we later learned that the following Tuesday was one of many holidays to which the Portuguese people are entitled and they take quite seriously. So, of course, the health center was closed.

Attempting again two weeks later, we entered the health center to find a raucous group: people of all ages and medical conditions standing in the entry way or sitting in the waiting room, waiting to be seen by the doctor or nurse. The administrative assistant had taken a break to get some coffee from a café down the road a bit; we'd have to wait to talk with her before we could proceed any further.

Despite our introductory letter translated into Google's best Portuguese, the keeper of the files and records was at a total loss as to what to do and how to process us … after all, we just didn't have the specific numbers her computer program required to grant us access to the sanctum sanctorum. After discussing our situation with other patients waiting to register for the doctor (or nurse), she picked up the phone and dialed someone somewhere … raising her voice with each question she asked and every answer she gave.

After hearing her say, "Bon, bom, obrigada, obrigada, ciao," she turned to me and managed to explain that we needed to go to the regional medical center in Alcains –

about a 15-minute drive – at 15:00 and ask for Sandra, who had been made aware of our circumstances.

Sandra knew exactly who we were and why we were there. But figuring out which boxes to tick and how to input our personal information was a challenge that required 30 minutes and the help of three other people seated with her in the reception area. Finally, the printer spat out two pieces of paper from which she cut off the bottoms, stamped each with a seal, and signed them. "That will be nine euros," she said – about U.S. $10. "€4.50 each for the doctor's consultation."

She also gave us forms whose many boxes were populated with numbers now. "The next time," she explained, "you will go to your own health center in Lousa and show them these papers. They will have the information they need, your 'números utentes,' to serve you there."

"Muito obrigados!" we replied, effusive in our gratitude.

The doctor, who had been sitting there throughout the entire episode, motioned us to follow her back to her office. Seated behind her desk, she entered our personal information into a computer and gathered each of our medicines needing refills. Click, click, click. Out from the printer came official forms containing our prescriptions.

We left the Alcains medical center and headed for the pharmacy, where we dropped off our prescriptions. They'd be ready for pick up the next day, the pharmacist explained in hesitant but understandable English. And the refills which the doctor had ordered? We could pick them up all together the next day … or wait and collect them month by month.

All told, we had prescriptions for 20 mg Cectoconazol (30 g) cream with three refills; fifty-six, 20 mg Omeprazol capsules (sold over-the-counter without a prescription in the USA), also with three refills; 120, 1 mg Alprazolam (generic Xanax) pills sold in "blister" packs, requiring a new prescription to refill; a blister pack of 60, 15 mg

Meloxicam pills; and another blister pack of 60 pills combining two separate prescriptions – 20 mgs + 15 mgs of Olmesartan medoxomilo + Hidroclororotiazida (one for high blood pressure, the other a diuretic) – also with three refills.

The combined cost for all these 13 boxes of medicines, some of which would last us for six months?

€51.

Just a little more than U.S. $61.00

And that's without insurance, co-payments, or deductibles … just our "números utentes."

The same supply of pharmaceuticals – even with Medicare or health insurance – would easily cost us at least hundreds of dollars in the USA.

Murphy and Me

"Anything that can go wrong, will go wrong."
Murphy's Law.

Named after Capt. Edward A. Murphy, an engineer working on a project designed to see how much sudden deceleration a person can stand in a crash, Murphy's Law and its corollaries explain why sh*t happens and causes the angst in our lives.

Especially in ours!

Like this, for example:

We purchased a 2012 Ford S-Max from a dealer in Cascais, a Lisbon suburb. It came with the standard, required, one-year guarantee.

Within weeks, both the "Engine Malfunction" and "Traction Control" warning lights came on, as the minivan lost almost all power.

Murphy's Corollary #1: "Whenever you set out to do something, something else must be done first."

We pulled off to the side and searched the manual downloaded earlier to our mobile (after discovering the printed manual in the glove box was purely in Portuguese. Even the diagrams!). In English, we read that the instrument cluster warning symbols alerted us to "stop driving and seek immediate assistance from a properly trained technician."

Immediately, we eased the car into the nearby underground parking area of the Allegro shopping mall center and left it there, locked. Friends drove us home.

Murphy's Corollary #2: "Nothing is as easy as it looks."

Not knowing anything about the technicalities and legalities that govern guarantees provided by (commercial) dealers selling used vehicles here in Portugal, we went online and Googled the Internet.

It didn't take long to discover some interesting information on an official European Union "Your Europe" website page:

"Q: If the product is defective, who is responsible for putting things right? A: The seller, even for purchases made on an internet platform."

Yeah, right.

Murphy's Corollary #3: "Everything takes longer than you think."

It was Saturday. Both the auto dealership and our insurance agency were closed. Wouldn't the weekend be when people had time to go shopping for cars and need insurance if they bought one?

Weird, huh? Welcome to Portugal!

We waited until Monday, then contacted the dealership in Cascais ... our insurance agent ... a towing company ... the local Ford dealership to alert them we'd be bringing the vehicle to them for diagnosis ... the area's only rental car agency ... and a taxi company, to pick us up and drive us around all these places in Castelo Branco.

Murphy's Corollary #4: "If there is a possibility of several things going wrong, the one that will cause the most damage will be the one to go wrong."

Later that day, the Ford technician contacted us with disturbing news: All four fuel injectors need to be replaced, at a cost of €1,500-€2,000. He attached an analysis and cost estimate to the email.

Murphy's Corollary #5: "Left to themselves, things tend to go from bad to worse."

We sent the report to the dealer who sold us and guaranteed the S-Max. We waited and waited for a reply. The dealer insisted that the repairs be made in Cascais ... and that we arrange to have the vehicle towed there.

The insurance company balked at towing it such a great distance.

Meanwhile, from the Ford dealership, we learned of other problems: When the mechanic opened the hood, he poked around and said to us, "The motor has rust. This is not good." He could offer no assurance that we wouldn't experience even more problems down the road.

Murphy's Corollary #6: "If everything seems to be going well, you have obviously overlooked something."

We contacted Cascais again, reviewing our experiences with the dealer and vehicle since purchasing it. Among them:

• The day after we got it, the air conditioner wouldn't work. Dealer said it was working when he drove the car. But a mechanic found only 10% of the "gas" necessary for the air conditioner to function. We paid €100 for the air conditioning system to be filled with gas and recharged.

• Admittedly, the hood insulation had somehow been broken, but we were promised that a new one would be delivered immediately to us. It never was, despite three emails to which we never received a reply. Only when threatening an official complaint was I told that the part would be delivered when, "a colleague would be in our area on other business." After all, "shipping it is very expensive."

Murphy's Corollary #7: "Nature always sides with the hidden flaw."

We believe we'd been sold a defective vehicle.

Deliberately, perhaps.

After the sale, the dealer certainly wasn't particularly cooperative. In fact, we still hadn't received our legal ownership papers for the S-Max!

If there are lessons to be learned here, I'd caution: (1) Be very careful when purchasing a car from a "virtual stand," where the dealer isn't a full-service dealership; (2) Never purchase a used vehicle until it's been inspected by a qualified, objective mechanic; and (3) Always purchase close to home.

We appreciated all the ideas, input, opinions, and feedback received from concerned folks via Facebook when we posted our problem.

So, add this corollary to Murphy's law: "Post a problem on Facebook and people will *Like* something that's terrible, comment with advice and admonishments, attribute any mistakes in what they've written to auto-correct, and insist that you've written too much."

Much ado about nothing?

That's William Shakespeare, not Murphy.

But between Murphy and me, the Bard never purchased a used car in Portugal!

"Dirty Water" and Other Cravings

Undoubtedly, I'm going to be crucified for my confessions here, so be my guest ... skip to the end of this piece ... and give it your best shots.

"What do you miss most from the USA?" I'm frequently asked.

Leading my list this morning is American-style coffee.

You know: what locals, especially, refer to as "dirty water."

Coffee is almost a religion in Portugal; but unlike religion, it's worshiped daily here. Both the Portuguese and Spanish are addicted to their bold beverage, which they drink from early in the morning until late at night. From Buondi to Ristretto Ardenza, the consistency of Portuguese coffee seems more like motor oil to me than the "pish" water we Americans drink and consider caffeine.

I'm not looking for that over-priced, sugary, syrupy Starbucks stuff that's more like make-believe ice cream dressed up as coffee ... but, please, let me find something akin to my mellow-morning-medium-roast-breakfast-blend: Folger's, Maxwell House, Chock Full O'Nuts. Costco's Kirkland brand.

Anything but "instant."

Along with the coffee, I yearn for my Keurig coffee maker. Krups makes something like it, known as "Dolce Gusto" (we have one!), but it's just not the same. Besides, the polluting plastic pods (Nescafé produces them for the Dolce Gusto) are more java-jolting than Green Mountain's ... whose name, at least, implies environmentally-friendly.

Apart from people, I guess what I miss most from the USA is its food.

Topping the chart is a real New York City Carnegie Deli-style sandwich piled high with spicy pastrami on rye bread with a shmear of mustard, some creamy cole slaw, a sour pickle, and cheese cake that adds pounds to your waistline just by admiring it. (Carnegie's has closed, but similar fare has been available at Katz's Delicatessen— since 1888!)

Bagels – even "plain" ones – though onion, garlic, cinnamon raisin, asiago cheese, and "everything" bagels would be seventh heaven … if they could be found (not frozen) within driving distance.

And steaks! Hunger-hunkering slabs of beef, perfectly cut with just the right amount of fat. Filet Mignon. Porterhouse. Rib Eye. Strip steak, flank steak, even top sirloin! I wonder whether those Kansas City mail order steak houses deliver to Portugal?

Other favorite foods that are hopefully hiding on shelves somewhere around these parts are grapefruit juice (found at Continente!); canned pumpkin (a great source of fiber without fat to bulk up your pet's food without adding weight to the animals); a wide(r) variety and selection of salad dressings – not just mayonnaise, olive oil, and vinegar, along with a token "ranch" – and Tabasco-style hot sauces (anything but Piri-Piri!) for Bloody Marys and Sunday brunches.

And restaurants …

What I wouldn't give for a Tex-Mex restaurant's multi-page menu featuring variations on the theme! They're probably there in the larger, more tourist-oriented cities. But what about Thai restaurants? Where are they hiding, apart from on the back pages of our Chinese restaurant menus? Speaking of Asian food, a Japanese restaurant couldn't hurt. Heck, sometimes I even grow nostalgic for IHOPs (although rumor has it their menu has changed from stacks of flapjacks and waffles to burgers and pizza), Baskin-Robbins, and Dunkin' Donuts.

Food may top my wish list, but there's lots more I wish we had here:

• Allergy pills that really work (there's so much pollen here!) … and Nyquil and/or Robitussin would be an added bonus;

- Aspirin: low dosage (81-100 mgs) sold in big bottles for a couple of bucks, rather than blister packets of 30 for > 4€;
- Automatic transmissions: especially when my vehicle is stopped, facing uphill with others behind, on particularly steep streets;
- Convenient conversion cards: to tell me how much something really weighs, how hot (or cold) it really is, how much it really measures, how fast my car is really moving, how much fuel my tank is really taking;
- Hot dogs, real hot dogs, not salchicas or those squiggly things they sell in a jar here. Nathan's Famous. Hebrew National. Even Ball Park franks will do nicely, thank you;
- Horseradish: the heavy-duty super-hot stuff that comes in jars … and bottles of crushed red pepper flakes … vanilla extract, too;
- Letter-size paper: 8.5 X 11 inch (no idea about converting that to cms) that will comfortably fit in my files and folders;
- Paper plates: not those plastic-coated imitations sold everywhere;
- Shark vacuum cleaners or anything that will suck up all that dust and dirt without requiring herculean strength;
- Prilosec (or its generic substitutes) without a prescription;
- Rachel Maddow: live on CNBC;
- Bookstores stocked with a good selection of English language books and magazines: Amazon (.es or .uk) is just too expensive;
- Really good bacon, Ritz or saltine crackers, and "ethnic" foods;
- The (complete) Sunday *New York Times;* and
- Toilet tissue: the soft and absorbent kind – not sand paper.

It's not that this stuff isn't available here … just daring to be found. Expensive, too, at times. But we make do, knowing that friends in the bigger, more affluent cities – Lisbon, Porto, Algarve – and their suburbs have stores that sell these staples. We've also discovered the GB Superstore that carries much of our heart's content, food-wise, at least. Though located in Cascais, outside of Lisbon, their website is a cornucopia of dietary delights … and they'll deliver or ship!

Lest anyone worry, rest assured that we're doing fine – really well –with what we do have here. And what we don't have? We probably don't need it, anyway. We're still newbies, who are learning to adjust.

Even to the coffee.

Despite being serious business in Portugal and Spain – an amphetamine and aphrodisiac of the gods to some – to me, coffee is just a beverage.

Blasphemy! Sacrilege! Heresy!

Now, let the carnage continue.

P.S. After writing this, I came across a Dolce Gusto representative handing out one euro discount coupons at Jumbo, a super supermarket here. She told me to try the "Sical" blend. Rated a "7" in terms of its strength (most other blends are 8-10), it isn't as potent as other choice flavors. Bingo! I'm now a convert (although it really isn't that much different from American dirty water). ☺

Super/Markets & Grocery Shopping

Since we all don't live on "quintas" and grow our own food, or belong to co-ops where we share that food with others (who share theirs with us), we are among those who purchase our food – along with personal products and household supplies – at local shops, grocery stores, and super/markets.

In Spain, every town of any size has at least one major supermarket (in addition to specialty shops: fruit and vegetable stands, butchers, bakers and bread shops, fish mongers, corner markets inserted between "bazaars," delicacy shops that we'd call delicatessens or delis in the USA ... although their foodstuffs are totally different).

Olvera, our hometown in southern Spain, has two: Dia (Distribuidora Internacional de Alimentación) which is known by its Minipreço ("Low price") brand name in Portugal ... and Mercadona, a larger, full-service supermarket with everything departmentalized under one roof, and an annoying jingle that gets under your skin, erupting when one showers, shaves, drives, or otherwise isn't thinking about grocery shopping.

Few Portuguese towns or villages have such supermarkets. Instead, the "corner" market is where one shops when you run out of something essential or forgot to buy it while at a city-sized supermarket. And when you want fresh rolls or bread baked that day (two lunch rolls are €0.32). Or when you want to shoot the breeze, brushing up on your Portuguese with neighbors who are also there buying a thing or two.

But for major shopping excursions and expeditions here, most head to Castelo Branco's industrial zone, where no fewer than five major supermarket chains have staked out territory alongside warehouse-size specialty stores selling breads, cheeses, fruits, and everything your pets and animals could possibly need (Agriloja).

We do our food and supply shopping weekly at these super/markets, visiting one or more frequently. Often back-to-back, on the same day.

While all of these mega-markets sell the same things (more-or-less), we've developed preferences for this place and that, according to the specific objects of our desire.

If empirical research is to be believed, first among equals is Jumbo, the anchor store at one of our two major malls here in Castelo Branco.

According to DECO, Portugal's largest (nonprofit) consumer association that's been accorded "public utility" status, after analyzing almost 600 supermarkets in 70 countries, Jumbo was found to have the lowest prices of all large chain stores—especially in central Portugal. Further, the consumer watchdog's research highlighted that Jumbo's prices tend to be best across-the-board in terms of both fresh and frozen products, groceries, personal care, and household products.

The study found that "Jumbo was top of the table when it comes to cheap prices," as reported the English online weekly *Portugal News.* "It was the number one choice for many shoppers in areas including Aveiro, Coimbra, Leiria, Lisbon, Setúbal, and Viseu."

I can understand that: we relate Jumbo to the ubiquitous discount Walmart Supercenters spread throughout the USA.

Except, more often than not, Jumbo is out of the products we want or need—especially when "on sale." After seven separate trips, I've yet to find Jumbo restocked with the large size of its own brand mouthwash (the blue one, not green) or Johnson & Johnson baby powder.

To realistically reflect the shopping tendencies of Portuguese families, Deco's research put together a "hamper" comprising 243 products: 38% were a store's own-brand products and 62% were branded.

We shop regularly at Jumbo and, while we find that it's the greatest numerator and common denominator in terms of one-stop shopping, we aren't always thrilled with our Jumbo purchases. To be fair, Jumbo is the only place that carries our preferred Noir dark chocolate; and its own mouthwash – at one-third the cost – comes closest to the world's leading brands in terms of swig and bang for the buck. Jumbo seems to have a larger, consistent selection of "international" foods, and is the only place we've found Ricotta cheese to make lasagna.

Trailing a close second to Jumbo in Deco's ratings is Continente, where "prices are, on average, two percent more expensive than Jumbo."

While we sometimes do our weekly shopping at the Continente mini-mall outside Castelo Branco's industrial zone, we're not that impressed. Except on some of the special deals offered – like tables and chairs – in front of the store itself. This particular Continente appears to have very narrow aisles and rows, compounded by the number of shopping carts left unattended while customers head for items located in other aisles. We find the largest selection of paper goods at Continente (especially boxed tissues), and it's the only place nearby that sells real, luscious grapefruit juice not from concentrate or watered down.

On the other side of the industrial zone is our second major mall, where Pingo Dolce ("Sweet Drop") supermarket serves as its anchor store. Contrary to Deco's research – which found Pingo's prices, on average, six percent higher than Jumbo's – we think much of the inventory at Pingo costs less. Do we do our major shopping there? No. But we do, especially, appreciate Pingo Dolce's pre-prepared, ready-to-eat servings from its café bar and (when available), its chicken and/or tuna spread submarine sandwiches. Hey, can you even buy the fixings of these tasty foot-longers for just €1.97 … let alone, spend time fixing them?

Largely due to "the prices of their fresh fruits and vegetables" and meat and fish supplied by external companies, and "therefore higher prices," Deco's survey found Intermarché, Minipreço, and Lidl to be the most expensive supermarkets.

But we believe that depends on what you're looking to buy and spend.

Take Lidl, for instance.

Nowhere else – not at Jumbo, Continente, Pingo Dolce, Minipreço, or Intermarché – could we find such a vast variety of freshly-baked breads and bread products (like the "misto" croissants of ham and cheese, or the chorizo-filled rolls), cooked on premises and put out, piping hot, while you're standing there. At lower prices than anywhere else. We think the cuts of meat at Lidl are closer to "American-style" than anywhere else, and prefer Lidl's ice creams over others. Lidl is the only supermarket in the area where we can find real charcoal briquettes.

At Lidl, we buy "real" orange juice from the freezer case, similar to Tropicana and Florida's Natural brands. Elsewhere, the orange juice is made from concentrate, sold in boxes or containers displayed on the shelves, and tastes more like Tang orange drink than real juice (zumo). The store's "Diez" cosmetics, groceries, paper products, and other products give the competition a marathon for our money.

What's more, shopping at Lidl is like going on a treasure hunt: you'll never know what you'll find – clothing to small appliances, hardware to DVDs and CDs – in its bin aisles. It's the closest we've come to finding close-outs carried by the likes of TJ Maxx, Tuesday Morning, or Big Lots here today, gone tomorrow, in Castelo Branco.

So much for plugging Lidl … except to say that we're glad there's a Lidl market not far from us in Spain, too, at Morón de la Frontera.

Contrary to Deco's claims, we've found the best buys and lowest prices on certain items – store-brand cleaning products and supplies, even wines at times – at Minipreço, directly opposite Continente. It's not a place to wander up and down the aisles. You can't. But to run in and pick up certain cheaply-priced items, Minipreço can't be beat.

(Unless, of course, Jumbo, Continente, or Lidl have those items on sale.)

And then there's Intermarché, part of the Minipreço

and Lidl troika.

Yes, it is higher priced, yet we spend more of our time and money at Intermarché than at all the other supermarkets.

One reason is its location: Yes, there's an Intermarché (attached to its sibling, BricoMarché) in Castelo Branco's industrial zone. But the one in Alcains is much closer to us and it's far more convenient to run out for something we "need" (or forgot) when the destination is ten minutes, not thirty, away.

A bit smaller and more intimate, we prefer the Intermarché snack bar in Alcains. We've enjoyed many a meal – Italian-style meatballs, pork tenderloin, skewered turkey with onions and peppers all deliciously wrapped in bacon – which we've then bought fresh from the butcher case to bring home and cook later.

Results of Deco's recent research were released in early June 2018.

Two types of consumers were profiled in the study: those who spend €150 a month on shopping, and those whose monthly shopping costs up to €400. "Those who spend more also save more," it concluded.

Russ and I do spend more than €400 each month on our supermarket shopping, so we should have saved enough to be able to enjoy eating out at one of the area's fine dining establishments … or catching a movie at the Cineplex in the mall followed by a full, food court meal … right around the corner from Jumbo!

Mall-Lingering and Other Reality-Check Observations

Shopping malls may be dying in the USA, but here in Portugal they're alive and kicking. In the "industrial" zone of Castelo Branco, the major city closest to our little village of Lousa, besides scores of "big box" stores, there are two – yes, two! – popular shopping malls.

One of them, "Allegro," is anchored by Jumbo, a major grocery store and supermarket that's the closest in concept here to Walmart, Sam's Club, and/or Costco. Jumbo has its own "little" box store attached which sells all different types of electrodomésticos (household appliances) at discounted prices. There's also a laundry opposite Jumbo, where you can have five shirts washed and ironed by hand for under $10.

The Allegro mall offers underground parking, as well as a food court comprising half a dozen or so eateries … a bowling alley, and a multiplex cinema showing the latest movies (often, American flicks with Portuguese subtitles).

Among the other stores ("lojas") in this two-story mall are an optician, a household goods shop not unlike World Bazaar or Pier One Imports, and a discount shoe store with an attractive selection for men, women, and children; a health "supplement" store, a pharmacy, and a unisex clothing store … as well as random pop-up kiosks.

Nearby is another shopping center, The Forum, which reminds me more of the stores populating malls in the USA when they were magnets attracting folks for shopping and socializing. With covered parking rather than underground, the Forum, too, has its own fabulous food court comprising nearly half of the upper level.

In addition to a host of delicious "fast-food restaurants" – our favorites are the kabob place (a complete meal with an overstuffed kabob featuring your choice of meat or chicken + French fried potatoes + a drink … that costs just five euros!) and a Brazilian-style barbecue grill – are among the options.

Out of nostalgia, on our first trip to the Forum, we ate at Burger King (there's a Subway sandwich shop there, too).

Not a good choice, all things considered.

Clustered around the food court topping the lower level are the types of shops I remember, that formerly filled our American malls: several franchised clothing stores, opticians, sporting goods shops, electronics and appliance dealers, footwear, booksellers, a gift shop or two, a place to buy religious icons and paraphernalia, a discount cosmetics shop, an ice cream parlor, and yet another shoe store.

Taking a trip to Allegro or the Forum is like returning to yesteryear, when America really was great. (Insider joke: "MAGA!") There are the throngs of window-shoppers, people queuing up to pay for their purchases, families and friends socializing, that made malls and shopping centers a normative chapter in American life.

Unlike the vacancies, closures, and ghetto-ization of malls happening in the USA, people in Portugal go there to shop and spend money—the heyday hallmarks of our former suburban centers ... before their anchor stores went bankrupt, drowning ancillary shops, closing the cineplexes, and leaving a few lonely holdouts hoping that things would turn around.

Other outposts drawing shoppers to the industrial zone are the car dealerships, "big box" stores, stand-alone "hiper" markets and major grocery stores, furniture emporiums, tire shops, linen outlets, and the largest Chinese bazaar of them all. There's also a second-hand furniture shop, as well as the manufacturing facilities that give the area its name. This is where we found the new kitchen showroom and production place where we ordered ours, choosing from a wide selection of cupboards and cabinets, drawer and door pulls, sinks and spigots, granite counters and back splashes, all shown to us by a knowledgeable and congenial young sales associate.

To my unindoctrinated eyes, one of the nicest things

about shopping in Castelo Branco is that consumers still have a choice of venues: the hustle-bustle crowds in these shopping centers don't necessarily compete with the more tranquil specialty shops along the avenues, side streets, and back alley hideaways where people still stroll, enjoy a cup of coffee, a couple of cervejas, or glass of wine at the outdoor cafés ... dining out or inside the plethora of family restaurants and chef-owned cuisines that haven't been gobbled up by the chains.

# # # # #

From the daily and mundane to more complex matters that we tend to take for granted, the ways people in one country do things often differ quite a bit from how they're done in another.

Take banking, for instance.

Checks are virtually unheard of here in Portugal. Instead, one does almost everything through "Multibanco" ATM machines. Bank ATMs do much more than disperse cash from your account, or allow you to move money from one account to another within the same bank. You can pay bills and/or transfer money to other people, businesses, and government agencies ... regardless of their bank. And those recurring charges—like your electric, water, car payment, insurance, and telecommunication bills? They're billed to and paid directly by the bank, without you needing to lift a finger. Forgotten your personal IBAN number? You can obtain it — as well as a history of your transactions, withdrawals and money deposited — electronically through your home computer or mobile device and, of course, the Multibanco!

Driving is another activity that's quite different here from there.

I'm not referring to which side of the road we drive on or where your vehicle's steering wheel and pedals are located. It's much more complicated than that.

Consider speeding ...

People where we live in Portugal tend to be either speed demons or slow pokes. They'll tailgate your butt before pulling away and leap-frogging several vehicles to get ahead of you (even if you're driving over the posted speed limit) … or they'll drive you bonkers because of their motorcycle-cum-cars with sewing machine engines that slow everyone down, since they just can't get up to and maintain speed.

Keeping up with (if not ahead of) traffic is the name of the game here. And, whether or not you're driving fast "enough," there are always those who want to drive faster. So, move onto those special "laggard lanes" on the right, where available, and allow others to pass you!

Speed "bumps" are serious here, big and high, rather than the puny strips usually found in the USA. Then there are those "rumble strips," urging you to slow down— especially when approaching a stop or yield sign. And, each time you enter a village on a paved, country road, heed the "Velocidad Controlada" signs. Exceed the designated speed limit and you'll automatically trigger a red traffic light. Those striped lines where passengers have the right-of-way to cross the street? They do! And roundabouts (???!!!) Personally, I loathe them; but many swear by them—no matter how convoluted or complex. Give me a good, old-fashioned red, green, and yellow traffic light any day—blinking or not!

As someone used to hustle-and-hurry, indoctrinated to the extent that slowing down is hard to do, some things are sometimes enough to push me over the edge. For the most part, I relish the slower pace of life here and slip into it with ease … but when a local Portuguese person or Spaniard sees a friend and stops to chat – in his car, in the middle of the road, for at least five minutes, with no concern for those in the queue behind – being "rich in time" shouldn't be an issue, but often it is.

Without rhyme or reason, and in no logical order, here are some other curious or odd observations we've noticed while living in Portugal and Spain, which make living here quite different than back in the colonies:

• Coin-chained supermarket carts cut down the clutter and damage caused by shopping carts abandoned, helter-skelter, in parking lots.

• I'm not particularly a fan of "soft" drinks or soda "pop." But, every so often I do crave a Coke or Pepsi. Sugar (not artificial sweeteners) is used here, although both Coke and Pepsi sell diet drinks here, as well. Likewise, I've yet to pick up a bottle or can of almost any condiment and found the equivalent of "High Fructose Corn Syrup" listed as an ingredient. Someone told me that such preservatives are prohibited here. But another remarked that these additives just go by different names. There are more than ninety legally acceptable names for MSG in Europe, for example. Nonetheless, forget about eating meals at "American times." Restaurants don't even open here for dinner before 7:00 PM … and few tables are taken earlier than 8PM (20:00).

• Food and drink beg mentioning the sensitive topic of tipping. In the USA, where restaurant workers and other service providers frequently earn less than the minimum wage, tipping is appreciated and practiced – especially for superior service – typically to the tune of 15%-20% of the bill. (Some restaurants now automatically add a "courtesy charge" gratuity to your tab.) While certainly appreciated, tipping isn't expected or necessarily proffered in the smaller towns of Spain and Portugal. Most people we know who do tip, will leave one euro or fifty cents for a €20-25 bill. Still, the workers are surprised … and genuinely grateful.

• Vehicle license plates ("tags") stay with the car in Portugal and don't change with each new owner. Look at the plate: you'll know the month and year when a vehicle was first registered and put on the road.

• Used cars come with an obligatory full year warranty in Portugal, rather than 30-60 days of "power train" coverage. But, there's more paperwork required before you drive a car off the dealer's lot: among other things, you'd best bring acceptable documentation attesting that there's adequate insurance coverage in effect on said vehicle.

• Pets need to wear seat belts when out in the car, driving with their families. It's the law here. We're not talking about those improbable imitations of baby car seats adapted to dogs (or cats), but a leash that attaches to your pet's collar on one end and gets inserted to the seat belt buckle/clasp on the other. There's plenty of leeway for the dogs to sit, stand, lie down, even roll over ... but they can't jump out the car window or bolt from a door that accidentally opens. Rather not tether them using these pet seat belts? Then, you'll need to transport them in appropriate pet carriers.

• People, by and large, tend to treat their pets (especially dogs) differently in Portugal and Spain than do Americans. It's not that they don't love them or consider them part of their families, it's just that the psychology – between both people and pets – differs from what we've been used to in the USA. We're the "Americanos" who walk their dogs on leashes and pick up after them, depositing their litter in refuse receptacle bins. Most small-town Portuguese and Spaniards open the door and let their dogs (and cats) out to roam the streets and take care of their business. After all, it's their business ... not theirs.

• Expanding into more personal hygiene, at the risk of being offensive, it behooves me to mention bidets and toilets. Most Americans know what bidets are, even if we find them somewhat redundant. All I will say is, "Try it, you'll like it." As regards the even more sensitive subject of toilets, let's just say that the paper here isn't what Charmin has led us to expect. Few small towns and villages here have plumbing that can accommodate anything other than human waste, which means that tampons, tissues, paper towels, and – sometimes, somewhere – even toilet paper must be disposed of alternatively (and appropriately).

• Houses shouldn't be money pits—so, people, not

houses, are heated and cooled. Why heat or cool an entire house, when we're occupying only certain rooms or areas? Unlike the USA, where whole houses often are "air conditioned" – heated or cooled – including rooms and spaces that aren't in use or occupied, Europeans use "inverter" units in separate rooms. When sleeping, the bedroom aircon is turned on. Feeling cold while entertaining company? Only wood burners or space heaters in the kitchen, dining area, and/or gathering space need to be operating, while the rest of the house isn't consuming energy. No need to keep a water tank heated—just heat the water when/if you need it. Gas-fired water heaters provide an unending stream of hot water (until the propane tank runs dry). Reason enough to consider an electric one!

• Mediterranean Europeans – those from Portugal, Spain, and Italy especially – enjoy their long lunch "hours." They wouldn't think of working on vacation days or many "ferias" and holidays celebrated throughout the year. Often, they don't begin work before 10:00 AM and pace themselves according to their internal dictates and physical needs, rather than external schedules and time clocks. Longer lunches and café culture are among the delightful differences here.

• Is Portugal alone among the Romance languages in the way it counts and designates days? Spanish, French, and Italian all have similar words for Monday (Lunes, Lundi, Lunedi) through Saturday (Sábado, Samedi, Sabato) and Sunday (Domingo, Dimanche, Domenica) … but, when it comes to Portuguese, except for the weekend (Sábado, Domingo), the "market days" of the week are determined by when they fall in terms of Sunday as the first day of the week: Segunda-feira (Monday), Terça-feira (Tuesday), Sexta-feira (Friday). It's a bit confusing to keep count!

• I'd be doing us all a disservice if not mentioning the need to come to grips with international weights and measures. With my trusted tape measure, I can deal with centimeters vs. inches. But I always go online to convert kilos to pounds and kilometers to miles. Forget about converting temperatures between Celsius vs. Fahrenheit. Nobody will ever convince me that an infernal 118°F isn't hotter than 48°C ... or that 0°C isn't colder than its 32°F equivalent!

• Bureaucracy is almost an art form here. Even Portuguese people and Spaniards can be caught by the labyrinthine and tortuous system administered by people to whom it seems to exist only to slow or – if at all possible – stop the cogs from grinding. But maybe as a retired person rich only in time, even this doesn't really rankle much.

On balance, our life here in Portugal and Spain is far more than can be distilled onto a spreadsheet. And that includes the people who have welcomed us in their village, town, and country with extraordinary generosity, and helped through the vagaries of the local systems by almost everyone simply by learning to ask for their help.

Yes, many things are different now to what we were accustomed in the USA, especially in one fundamental respect: Here, people are human first and "nationals" only occasionally. Especially expats. Which is why we moved here.

What more can one ask for ... or is, ultimately, needed?

The Costs of Living

All things considered, the cost of living in Portugal or Spain is reasonable.

"Reasonable?" you ask. "I thought you said that the quality of life is high, while the cost of living is low in both countries."

Relatively speaking, that's true. But I must qualify.

The cost of a home – whether house, apartment, flat, "quinta," or land – is cheaper ... unless you're buying in a gold coast city: Lisbon, Porto, the Algarve coast; Barcelona, Ibiza, Madrid, etc. Purchasing that home, however, is more expensive in Spain than in Portugal because the "closing costs" on property in Spain include an 8% tax plus approximately U.S. $3,000 in administrative and legal-related fees (v. taxes beginning at 0.1% and settlement-related fees less than U.S. $2,000, by-and-large, in Portugal).

Similarly, the annual property taxes here in Iberia are far friendlier than those assessed in the USA.

We paid about $2,500 per year in NE Wisconsin (more, elsewhere in Wisconsin) for a property assessed at $130,000. When we lived in Florida (Jacksonville) and Virginia (Staunton and Manassas), annual property taxes were higher.

Our annual property tax in Portugal?

Just €135 (about $160).

In Spain, we're paying somewhere around $150 (€128) in property taxes each year on our "vacation bolt."

Much as some jurisdictions in the USA do, Portugal and Spain also charge taxes each year on such personal property as vehicles, boats, and aircraft based (more or less) on a factor of the property's value.

There's also IVA, that "value-added tax" surcharged throughout much of the European Union ... which can cause the price of goods and services to skyrocket. Unlike sales tax in the USA – which, even in the highest-cost areas, is under 10% — IVA can add 23% (Portugal) and

21% (Spain) to the price of your purchases. Since IVA taxes usually are already included in the cost, however, we're not that aware of them as taxes ... only that things don't cost as little as we'd expected.

Insurance on our homes and our cars, comparatively, is much lower here: Annual property insurance costs us about €250 ($300) in Spain and €200 ($235) in Portugal. Considering that we now only have one vehicle to insure (a 2012 Ford S-Max minivan), our annual auto insurance runs us €360 ($425) in Portugal, compared to the $1,250 (€1,065) we paid in Wisconsin to insure two cars per year.

As for health insurance, for far better and more inclusive coverage than in the United States, we pay €1,850 ($2175) per year in Portugal for two people – one 70, the other 55 – which is just about what it cost the younger of us to pay three monthly installments on his USA health care. Not only does our insurance cover us for sudden illness and accidents abroad (worldwide) for trips up to 60 days – including travel to the United States – it also pays a daily "subsidy" of €75 per day (after four days) for up to 120 days if either of us is incapacitated. The policy also comes with something called "Best Doctor Cover," an international network of the world's best specialists, for which up to €1,000,000 will be paid for serious illnesses: cancer, neurosurgery, coronary diseases requiring bypass surgery, stroke, and organ transplant. All expenses for inpatient, treatments, surgeries, doctor fees, other hospital services, travel of the insured person and a companion are covered!

Nevertheless, we haven't found that much of a difference in the costs of doing shopping in Portugal or Spain vs. the USA.

Some things – cosmetics, furniture, clothing, even linens – cost just as much (or more) as back in the USA. Ironically, we paid half of Portugal's price in Spain for 100% cotton bath towels that carried a "Made in Portugal" label.

Depending on where and what you're eating,

restaurants can cost a little less, a little more, or about the same in Portugal as in the USA. It's here that Spain and its tapas rule! Technically translated as "small plates," Spanish tapas frequently are filling enough for a meal … especially as preceded by olives, peanuts or potato chips and served with salad, vegetables, and bread. All for €2-€4 per plate!

For life's essentials and necessities – bread and water and milk, public transportation, health care and pharmaceuticals – prices in Spain and Portugal are more than modest … they're absolute bargains!

Sung by Amália Rodrigues is "Uma Casa Portuguesa," a fado from which these lines are taken:

> *Numa casa portuguesa fica bem*
> *Pão e vinho sobre a mesa*
> *E se à porta humildemente bate alguém,*
> *Senta-se à mesa com a gente*
> *Fica bem essa fraqueza, fica bem,*
> *Que o povo nunca a desmente*
> *A alegria da pobreza*
> *Está nesta grande riqueza*
> *De dar, e ficar contente*

Loosely translated, the sentiments speak much about what's truly valuable in life for the Portuguese:

> *In a Portuguese house, it is well*
> *Bread and wine are on the table*
> *And if someone humbly knocks on the door*
> *S/he will be invited to sit at the table with us*
> *Such sincerity and openness is a good thing, it is good*
> *That people are never denied or turned away*
> *The joy of poverty*
> *This is truly the greatest wealth*
> *To give is to be content*

Living with less, yet not worrying about being without life's basic essentials, is part of what it means to be an American expat yet live as the Portuguese or Spanish.

Friends often ask us, "So, how much does it cost to live in Portugal?" while other folks already living here are curious about how much they spend compares with what others are spending each month.

After some initial major, one-time outlays that aren't recurring, we have been able to determine our monthly living expenses and budget what it costs us to live here in Portugal.

Hopefully this will prove helpful to some of you.

When evaluating and comparing our expenses to yours, please consider that: (1) We live in a relatively lower-cost area of Portugal (a small village in the Castelo Branco metropolis ... not Lisbon, Porto, Algarve, etc.); (2) Without a mortgage or car payments, we are relatively debt-free; and (3) We don't live on a quinta or off the land. In fact, we have no land at all ... just a good-size property with nine good-sized rooms. We have two separate 30-AMP meters running our all-electric house.

Our monthly budget:

- €150 Electricity*
- €30 Water
- €140 Petrol/Gasoline for the Car
- €55 High-Speed Internet/TV/Telephones
- €15 Property Taxes
- €10 Vehicle Taxes
- €150 Health Insurance for Two (via afpop)
- €50 Insurance: Car (€30)/Property (€20)
- €500 Food: Groceries & Restaurants
- €100 Miscellaneous (Unbudgeted)
- €1,200 Total Monthly Budgeted Expenses

That's just about U.S. $1,375 per month (based upon the current TransferWise exchange rate).

Even if we inflate our cost of living in Portugal by 20%

across-the-board, we're looking at about €1,450 ... less than U.S. $1,675 ... still a "steal" ... as long as Congress continues to pay out its Social Security obligations.

Of course, others can pinch pennies and pence much better than we do and are far more frugal than us. As an example, a friend on Facebook compared his monthly outlays to ours:

- €35 Electricity
- €0 Water (There are no water meters in their village yet)
- €0 Propane/Butane for Water Heating (They pay €0 for solar heat)
- €150 Petrol/Gasoline for the Car (Diesel)
- €90 High-Speed Internet/TV/Two Mobiles + One Home Telephone
- €6 Property Taxes for One House and One Workshop
- €10 Vehicle Taxes
- €0 Health Insurance for Two (They're "optimists," they admit.)
- €15 Insurance: Vehicle Only
- €200 Food: Groceries & Restaurants (plus garden produce)
- €100 Miscellaneous (Unbudgeted)
- €496 Monthly Budgeted Expenses

WOW! That's just about a third of what we're spending.

I'm sure not making any judgment calls here – "different strokes for different folks" – but it's amazing to know that one can live (so) well here in Portugal on (so) little.

Our house is relatively large (125m2) by Portuguese standards. We have four "inverter" units heating or cooling the rooms that we occupy ... four dehumidifiers removing interior moisture to minimize mold, mildew, and the "damp" ... two water heaters serving two kitchens and two baths. Other electric appliances include a refrigerator, freezer, and counter-top fridge ... plus a washer that cleans several loads each week, and a dryer used when inclement weather makes it the only way to dry our wash.

Moving Money

Quick: How much is a euro worth?

That depends upon whose value you're comparing it to—and when.

Let's say, the American (U.S.) dollar. Today.

So, how much is a euro worth, in terms of the U.S. dollar, today?

Google: "Convert U.S. dollars to euros." You'll get a number of results, including the official exchange rate. But what you see isn't at all what you'll get. Because the "official" exchange rate doesn't include such margins as bank fees, transfer charges, and different conversion ratios for individual consumers vs. larger businesses and governments.

Any number of financial instruments and institutions we've taken for granted function quite differently outside the USA ... and some adjustments need to be made along the way when moving abroad.

Do/will/can you maintain a bank account – savings, checking, money market, etc. – in the USA while living elsewhere? Check with your financial institutions as to whether they'll allow you to keep an account with them. Without a U.S. address on record, two banks refused to retain our accounts. That wasn't a problem, however, for either of our credit unions, located in separate states.

Once determined that you can keep your account, ensure that you can employ the bank's bill payer service if you have a "foreign" address. If not, you may want to create a direct "external transfer" between banks that do and don't, so that your bill payer service remains active.

Even when changing your address to outside the USA, you may still need to provide periodic "travel alerts" to your bank(s) – every three months or so – to maintain account access.

Travel alert notices need to be submitted for all the credit (and debit) cards you'll be using abroad, too, which makes this an ideal time to reconsider which credit cards best suit your spending and serve your needs. Many, for instance, offer bonus mileage, other "rewards," or a percentage of money credited back for your purchases ... although they may also levy stiff "international transaction" fees on your purchases.

We've found the best all-around credit card for us is Bank of America's Travel Rewards: no annual fee, no international transaction charges, and 1% back on all purchases we make. Plus, travel alerts can be initiated and updated by card holders conveniently online.

Many of us use our debit cards at the ATMs in Portugal and Spain to withdraw money. Save some money: Insert your card in the machine, confirm your password or access code, and indicate how much cash to withdraw. You'll then be presented with a screen asking whether to accept the dollar amount shown that your account will be charged. For instance, withdraw €100 and the screen may ask you if you're willing to have your bank charged, say, U.S. $124.18 for the transaction. You'll be asked to confirm your choice before the cash is disbursed.

In our experience, we always have done better – by at least ten euros per hundred dollar transaction – when we don't agree to that dollar amount to being deducted from our bank account. We choose the euro option and allow our home bank to assign the transfer rate. It's easy to see how much money has been deducted for the transaction online.

Amazon gift cards technically aren't "credit" or "debit" cards, but family and friends often give them as gifts to their international loved ones. Unfortunately, cards from Amazon.com generally can't be used for purchases anywhere but in the USA. Although Amazon is a global enterprise and your account – even "Prime" memberships – can travel around the world with you, your purchases can't. Amazon is sort of a franchise: certain benefits convey country to country, and others not. Amazon.es (serving Spain and Portugal) won't accept your Amazon.com gift cards. And you can't "trick" Amazon.com (U.S.) or

Amazon.co.uk (Britain) to sell you something that cannot be shipped to Portugal or Spain due to delivery and customs clearance challenges.

Do you have a taxpayer number (NIF in Portugal; NIE in Spain)? You really can't do anything of financial consequence without having this identifier. Fortunately, it's simple enough to obtain—a designated fiscal representative (attorney, family member, trusted friend) can secure one on your behalf ... even while you're still in the USA.

Don't be surprised when a cashier asks, "Numéro de contribuinte?" (Taxpayer number?) while you're checking out and paying for purchases in Portugal. By and large, you're not required to provide it; but they're obligated to ask if you want to have it recorded and filed.

How much money you'll receive when you transfer funds from the USA to a euro bank account (or vice-versa) depends upon the exchange rate. And how the funds are being transferred. Ironically, you'll get more of (and for) your money going through a "middle man," than by sending funds between banks.

Currency exchange services save you money by negotiating a rate of exchange directly from the currency trading floor. Due to continuous fluctuation in currency rates, banks set their rates every morning to ensure that, no matter what rate they give you, they will never be left short. (You'll notice that banks offer a high rate to sell and a low rate to buy; they're covering the eventuality of daily currency movements.)

With dozens of currency exchange services out there, which one will give you the biggest bang for your bucks?

Do your homework and the arithmetic, as it often comes down to personal preference or whether you're a "preferred" client based on the value of past dealings. With large currency transfers – for example, when we purchased our homes in Portugal and Spain – we found our best deals from Global Currency Exchange Network (GCEN: gcen.co.uk). For the monthly transfers of Social

Security payments deposited into our U.S. bank account, we are especially satisfied with the rates and prompt services of TransferWise (transferwise.com). With an exchange rate of 0.88710 on a recent $1,000 transfer to euros, we saved $74.22 on the transaction compared to banks.

What about interest and fees here from your EU bank?

That depends on the bank and the account(s) you have there. But, typically, you'll notice more deductions – "fees-for-services" – charged by the bank to serve as a clearing house for your bills, payments, and fund transfers.

Don't forget to check your account activity periodically online: your bank accounts, credit and debit cards. How often? Whatever works best for your personal comfort level. In a world of political, economic, and cyber insecurities, I check ours at least twice weekly.

Tips on Gratuities

Here's a sensitive topic if there ever was one: tipping.

That extra "something" provided to (certain) people who provide services to us: waiters and waitresses, barbers and hair stylists, guides, helpers and assistants working for contractors you're paying directly.

I've asked the question(s) many times of lots of people. And plenty, in turn, have asked me: Do you tip? Who(m)? Where? How much?

Unlike USA workers in some industries and trades, tips aren't necessarily expected by their counterparts in Portugal and Spain.

But they're surely appreciated … especially if unanticipated.

There's a theoretical irony here in that a "tip," according to reasonable references, was originally given "to insure promptness." Promptness? Doesn't that go against the grain here in Portugal and Spain?

But the reasons for gracious tipping these days go well beyond timing and promptness. They're about the quality of service we've received.

Regardless of where they're working or what they're doing in their jobs, my understanding is that Portuguese and Spanish workers are entitled, at least, to the prevailing minimum wage.

Not so in the "colonies," where restaurant and salon workers (among others) are paid a lower minimum wage, often not even earning enough to cover the basic costs of living. For them, tips comprise a substantial portion of their income.

In Spain and Portugal, people in these same fields of endeavor make little more (if any) than the legal minimum wage. As of January 2018, that's €676.67 (U.S. $787.14) per month in Portugal and €813 (U.S. $998.71) in Spain— although Spain's minimum wage went up to €900 ($1,028) in 2019.

Despite the lower costs of some products and services

here on the Iberia peninsula, I couldn't live on those wages. Could you?

So, yes, I tip. Because I feel good when I can help and give a little extra.

But only for good and/or special service. And, usually, not to the owner or proprietor of a business, even if s/he is the one who is serving me … although, contrary to the conventional rule not to, I do tip taxi drivers who help me load and unload lots of baggage to and from airports.

Not everyone tips. They just don't believe in it, as it's not part of their culture, upbringing, and overall formation. If and when they do tip, it's typically given as a token— but appreciated, nonetheless.

Tipping has been one of those difficult adjustments for me to make, now that we live in Portugal and Spain.

While I am tempted to use the same rule of thumb that guided my gratuities in the USA – 20% for superior service, 10-15% for satisfactory, less for less – I am seeing how awkward even appreciative workers may feel and react when given a tip based on percentages such as these.

On a restaurant tab of, say, 20 euros, most service staff are delighted to receive a one euro (5%) tip … they seem uncomfortable accepting more: three euros (15%) or four (20%). Evidently, the rule of thumb is 5% in restaurants here and 10% only if lots of plates are being changed. Similarly, my barber is very grateful when I give him (or her) a 50 cent or one euro tip on a charge ranging from €6-10. More often than not, a few coins are appropriate and thankfully welcomed. Especially for beer or wine, coffee, and "raciones" (tapas).

When you do tip, try to leave it directly for those who have served you. In cash (or coins), not on credit or debit cards, whose transaction fees and merchant charges will be deducted from your largesse.

Ultimately, tipping – like most perks and bonuses – is a judgment call.

There's no right or wrong, no rules or standards set in stone.

My advice about tipping, therefore, is to do what feels right for you. Tip or don't tip, whenever, wherever, whatever you believe is appropriate.

Date Night Duos

Together with another couple, we enjoyed a date night for the first time since moving to Portugal.

Oh, the delicious irony of it all:

Watching a top-rated, first-run, American-produced movie based on a Swedish pop group, comfortably seated in a climate-controlled cinema in Portugal … listening to dialogue and music in English, while watching subtitles roll by in Portuguese … and understanding enough of the two languages to consider the accuracy and quality of the translation. Without missing a beat!

But, first, enjoy food from a variety of vendors.

It's called "Cinema + Jantar" here at the Allegro shopping mall in Castelo Branco. Between Sunday and Thursday, it costs only nine euros per person for the movie and the meal. That's just about U.S. $10.

Throughout Portugal, restaurants and cinemas in shopping centers are teaming up to offer special deals like this. It's a win-win for all!

Where and when can one see a newly released movie in the USA these days for less than ten dollars (except for specific "senior citizen" show times and/or intervals when the theater is otherwise vacant)?

Whoever wrote the advertising copy for this film-and-fest could have worked for me at my public relations and marketing firm:

"Onde alguns ouvem Cinema e Jantar, outros ouvem encontro romántico, saída com os amigos, ou tempo a sós. A verdade é que ninguém quer ser a pessoa com a barriga a dar horas no momento mais tenso do filme."

Rough translation: "Where some like the idea of a Movie and a Meal, others are enticed by a romantic encounter, going out with friends, or spending quality time by oneself. The truth is, no one wants to be the one with the grumbling tummy at the most inopportune moments of the film."

(What's not mentioned is that what's referred to here is

a seven-minute intermission during the film when you can get something to eat or take care of business, whatever it is.)

Regarding the sponsors:

Four different restaurants – each with great food – have prime roles in the dining experience: a pizza parlor, barbecue den, hamburger haven, and "piglet border" (leitão beirão)—which is why we never should fully trust Google to handle our translations correctly. At each eating place, you'll choose a main course, side dish, and a beverage.

Between us, we enjoyed some of the best burgers in town, pork BBQ sandwiches, and a pretty darned good pizza loaded with lots of fixings. The sides – hand-cut potato chips – weren't the greatest, but none of us were disappointed with our beer or wine … until our female friend gave me that evening's Portuguese lesson, correcting my pronunciation of the word for wine (vinho):

"It's VEE-N-YO," she demonstrated, upper teeth deliberately touching her lower lip, to correct my hitherto Spanish pronunciation of the word (vino): "BEE-NO," lips vibrating, but teeth never touching the lip.

But, back to the show:

We saw *Mama Mia II (Here We Go Again)*, which was wonderful … despite my frustration that nobody (except me) stood up to sway and swing and clap along with the music. The Portuguese, at least those attending that performance of the show, were much more constrained and sedate—although an elderly couple sitting opposite us sort of-kind of waved their arms in the air.

Showcasing a vintage Cher and Meryl Streep, the prequel-sequel movie ended with us in joyful tears, a moment blissful grace.

Words from the sponsors?

"Let yourself be swept away by the flavors and the plot."

Climax and conclusion:

"There are happy endings that cost only nine euros."

Exit, stage left. And roll the credits …

Partners

"The people of Portugal don't judge a person's sexual orientation but, rather, his or her character," a wise woman said to me.

As hate crimes continue to escalate in the USA and same-sex marriage, though now the law of the land there, faces renewed opposition and denials by government employees – clerks of the courts – responsible for granting marriage licenses to qualified applicants, I am reminded of yet another reason why we love Portugal and Spain.

Sexual orientation and gender identity don't appear to be issues here.

Whether the people are predisposed with preconceived notions about another's primal behavior, I haven't noticed a preoccupation with the nature of personal relationships or prejudicial attitudes about intimate involvements.

In fact, the entire nomenclature – the words we use to identify and call this or that – takes a bit getting used to and understanding.

Take "partner," for instance. Despite its business associations and financial connections, it's my own preferred word to describe a relationship in which we share the substance of our lives together.

Evidently, others feel the same way, too.

We've met more married couples here who refer to their spouses as "partners" rather than husband or wife. The same goes for committed couples who, but for common law, aren't technically married.

And, although I advocate gender-neutral vocabulary whenever possible (and practical), "spouse" simply doesn't convey that warm-and-fuzzy feeling as does "partner" (or husband and wife, for that matter).

"Mate" can also be gender-neutral, but no longer implies what it did. Once upon a time – for many Americans, at least – one's mate referred to one of a pair: either member of a couple and especially a married couple, or either member of a breeding pair of animals, or either of two matched objects—like socks. A sexual connection was often implied or inferred when referring to someone as your mate. Not anymore: that's archaic. Now, especially among Brits, "mate" is more commonly used as a familiar form of address—as in "friend" or "buddy."

Except when paired with soul, as in "soulmate."

My mother-in-law – bless her heart – introduced us to her friends as "soulmates." When we told her we preferred "partners," she shook her head and wouldn't hear of it. "No," she insisted. "You're soulmates!"

At the time, same-sex marriage was verboten, unlawful in the USA. So, when we took a Mediterranean cruise around Spain – where same-sex marriage already was legal – we considered asking the ship's captain to do the honors. It would be largely ceremonial, since none of the rights and responsibilities of a "real" marriage would be recognized by the governments of the USA.

Later, we celebrated at a recommitment ceremony in Spain, where I had the honor and pleasure of marrying another man and a woman – two of our very close friends – at the same time. Not only was the wedding and marriage recognized legally in the United States, but in Spain and Portugal … and lots of other countries, too.

How ironic that two of the most "Catholic" countries in the world – Portugal and Spain – were in the forefront of recognizing both civil and human rights, regardless of the church's official teaching and position.

Attraction, like emotion, is legitimate but not logical … less a product of the mind than what abides in our hearts and hormones.

So, whatever term of endearment – partner, spouse, mate, husband, wife – you're most comfortable with when referring to that special companion in your life is yours to choose and use.

Yet, how does that play out among the Spanish and Portuguese, who refer to their intimate relations as "esposo" and "esposa" (husband and wife, in both languages), but "marido" and "mujer" ("mulher" in

Portuguese)? The man is a husband in both countries; but the wife is referred to as (my) "woman." Both countries are rather progressive, yet with remnants of provincial sexism and ownership.

And what about the symbols: Does it matter on which finger, left hand or right, a wedding ring is worn anymore—if at all? Or who does the gardening and who cleans the house? Who takes the kids to school and who stays home to care for them when they're sick?

"It's a bit of contradiction that Portugal is generally very progressive on sexual orientation but quite sexist in daily business dealings," noted one male observer. "When we go to the bank, they automatically speak primarily to me, even if my wife speaks first, put my name first even when asked not to, etc. In one store, my wife handed a credit card to the owner, he ran it and then handed it to me. We have plenty of other examples, but it is odd. Fortunately for us, Portugal treats race the same way as sexual orientation and we have run into no issues with that, unlike in the U.S."

A Portuguese woman noted, "I am divorced and all the goods, savings and property were divided 50% for each part." Shen quickly added, "The problem in Portugal, in my opinion, is child support after the divorce ... that is a real problem."

So, do the same standards hold true for the Portuguese people and Spaniards today? Look around: Depending on where you live, the answers may vary. Or maybe they won't.

You'll need to get to know your neighbors better.

Which is how it should be, anyway.

Just don't intrude or interfere!

For Better and for Worse ...

Partner, mate, significant other, other half (or better) all are words we commonly use to connote a special commitment between two people who have chosen to pursue a life together.

But for those seeking the state's full and complicit recognition of their relationship, only marriage will do. For better or for worse, it's a status laden with directives handed down from on high by religious orders, civil authorities, and public policies.

And while marriage is a sacred trust, a "sacrament," as some churches call it, peculiarities portuguêsas and eccentricities españolas make it a miracle that expat marriages even occur on the Iberia peninsula.

Those wanting to wed in Portugal have two choices: A Catholic Marriage. Or a civil (secular) one.

Everything else is an afterthought.

To be binding under Portuguese law, if you want to have a "religious" wedding but don't follow the Catholic faith, you'll first need to undergo a civil ceremony. Meanwhile, residency restrictions and administrative formalities governing civil ceremonies sway many American expats or foreign nationals to go the route of a religious ceremony in Spain.

For a civil ceremony in Spain, at least one of you must be a Spanish citizen or a legal resident for two years prior to the wedding day. Other options are to get married elsewhere and have your wedding ceremony blessed in Spain ... or to cross the border into Gibraltar, where conjugal requirements are less stringent.

Jewish, Islamic, and Protestant wedding ceremonies are legally recognized in Spain; and, unlike Portugal, a civil marriage is *not* required a priori to one conducted outside the Catholic faith.

The Portugal Civil Registry Code, as does its Spanish counterpart, has overall requirements one must satisfy to be married:

- You must be at least 18-years old—with parental consent, however, you can marry if you're 16 or 17;
- The bride and groom must not be related;
- You need to request a license from a Civil Registrar Office in Portugal or Spain, and indicate whether the marriage will be performed under civil codes or religious beliefs;
- There's a waiting period while the announcement of your intention to marry is posted and made available for the public to comment; and
- Portugal wedding ceremonies must be in Portuguese, with at least two witnesses watching (language isn't an issue in Spain, where only one witness who's not related is required).

Under U.S. law, diplomats and consular officers are not permitted to perform marriages, nor can they be performed on the premises of U.S. embassies or consulates.

Same-sex marriages have been allowed in Portugal since 2010 and offer equal rights to the couple regarding property, taxes, and inheritance … since 2016, married couples of the same sex can also adopt and foster children. (Spain legalized same-sex marriage in 2005, along with its adoption rights.)

While there are no residency requirements to get married in Portugal, one of you must be in the country a minimum of thirty (30) days before notice of your proposed marriage can be given.

The marriage route is long and tedious in both Spain and Portugal, usually taking a minimum of four weeks just to process an application. After you have received approval to get married, the wedding can then be arranged … as long as it takes place within three months.

Documents must be obtained and presented to the Civil Registry where the wedding will occur, as well as taken with you on your wedding day to the place where you will marry. The documents must be original, either endorsed with an Apostille or authenticated by a licensed Notary Public. Official translations undertaken by authorized

agencies must accompany all these documents if they're not in Portuguese or Spanish:
• Certified birth certificates issued within six months;
• Passports (and/or residence permits);
• A "Certificate of No Impediment" (except for British nationals) from the local registry office in your Portuguese town or at an embassy for a civil wedding, or by a parish priest for a Catholic one. This document can't be issued by the U.S. Embassy, as, "no such document or governmental authority exists to issue it," explains the U.S. Department of State. "However," it notes, "you can execute a statement of eligibility to marry at the U.S. Embassy in Lisbon before a consular officer and present it to the Civil Registry office." Similarly, "No document equivalent to Spain's *Fe de Solteria y Vida* (Certificate of Existence and Civil Status) exists in the United States." According to the State Department, "Spanish authorities will accept a sworn statement from a U.S. citizen, affirming that he/she is single and free to marry, if executed before a U.S. Consular Officer";
• Proof of residency, a Spanish town hall certificate attesting that you've lived in the area at least two years. Although that isn't required to marry in Portugal, you should be able to prove that you've been in the country at least 30 days prior to the marriage;
• Final divorce papers, if applicable, apostilled and translated into Portuguese or Spanish within the last six months. If your marriage wasn't canonically annulled, you cannot be married in the Catholic church in either country;
• If applicable, the death certificate of your prior spouse, translated and apostilled within the last six months.

Want to be married in a Roman Catholic church? You also will need to provide official copies of your baptismal certificate.

Legal marriages contracted abroad generally are valid everywhere. Regardless of your residency status, if you're a "foreigner" in Portugal or Spain, though, remember to register the marriage with the country's consulate and with the local Civil Registry where you're now living.

An "interdenominational" pastor, I have been asked to officiate at weddings in Spain and Portugal.

One was a recommitment ceremony celebrating 30 years of marriage; another was a repeat performance of nuptials conducted days earlier in another country. Technically, both of these marriages already had taken place and, therefore, were recognized in Spain and Portugal.

So, there was no question about my pastoral propriety to pronounce the couples lawfully married.

Not that it mattered. It was pure pomp and circumstance for the "newlyweds," who wanted a ceremony to share their joy with others who couldn't be present to participate at the first, faraway wedding.

Standing before God as we witnessed and affirmed the sanctity of their marriages, it made no difference what the government thought or said. We were responding to a higher authority, seeking a blessing to live happily ever after.

Vacation

We'd spent the last five years on the road, looking at properties in southern Spain and central Portugal. Then, we jumped through hoops and sustained hoopla to ensure our purchases were bona fide … and that we'd be granted governmental permission (visas!) to live there. More recently, we worked with contractors to make the repairs and rehabs deemed necessary to turn abandoned houses into our homes.

Five months after arriving in Portugal and finishing much of the work on our property in Lousa, Castelo Branco, we decided to take our three dogs with us on a "real" vacation and see some of the sights (and sites) we'd thus far only posted Thumbs Up! *Likes* on Facebook pictures.

Our time away would be short (just six days) and our agenda agreeable: We'd stay somewhere near the beaches north of us, close to the coast, with easy access to Portugal's convenient train system. From there, we'd take day trips: Monday's market at Espinho, a gondola ride in Alveiro, the extraordinarily tiled buildings (especially the church) of Ovar, and a day sampling some of Porto's special deliciousness.

Searching the listings on Airbnb, FlipKey, and TripAdvisor, we found what sounded like the perfect place: a "romantic room in a magic place near the beach," the property touted its "artistic atmosphere." Offering "lots of privacy," it was in front of the train station – just ten minutes to Porto! Amenities included bed linens and bathroom towels, WiFi Internet, a private garden, and a kitchen with fridge, stove, toaster, and kettle. Plus, among the property's features was its waterfront location!

The sole drawback (for us) was that its one-and-a-half bathrooms would be shared.

The place had been booked continuously, from April through October, according to its hosts. But with a bit of shuffling, six days were available toward the end of

August. I contacted the property's lister with a bunch of questions: Would three dogs be acceptable? Was it a non-smoking property? How would sharing the bathroom(s) actually work?

"No problem at all," she replied. "Just enjoy."

Before losing our chance at what appeared to be a place ideally suited for us, I confirmed the reservation and paid by credit card.

Hindsight, at best, is 20/20. But using a credit card is paying it forward!

"Don't you think it's a little strange that, with all those bookings, there's not even a single review for this place?" Russ asked me. Not one guest had taken a moment to say something – good, bad, indifferent – about their experience there. Most properties had a fair share of comments. Not this one, though.

That should have been a harbinger.

We packed the car and spent about €50 in tolls and a tank full of gas before pulling up and parking in front of the property.

"Is this it?" I asked, incredulously. There's always one derelict property surrounded by others in pristine condition. Ours was the destitute one.

Blue boards tried valiantly to look like a cross-weave pattern through which weeds wound their way up, down, and through the broken wooden remnants. An unlatched double gate, painted the same color blue, was opening and closing on one side, blown by the breeze.

From the exterior, at best it could be thought of as a "beach house" … but the word that stuck in my mind was "ramshackle." Nowhere to be seen was a beach, let alone the promised waterfront.

Facing the house was the train station. Every ten minutes, sometimes sooner, we'd hear the tick-tick-tick-tick signaling an approaching train, followed by a series of bells, as the guard rails came down. Local commuter trains. Freight trains. Express train service between Porto and Lisbon. All stopped or sped by, clickity-clack, clickity-clack on the tracks, as the transports tooted, honked, squealed, and blared off-key melodies announcing their every approach and departure.

While Russ – with some help from the property agent and her artist – emptied the car and carried in our bags, I walked the dogs.

Our amiable hosts apologized when the bedroom's inside door knob kept falling off and onto the floor, explaining that the property wasn't actually theirs—they rented it from the owner, who had been negligent in his responsibilities regarding its upkeep.

Although the description specifically stated that the property's two-bedroom, one full and one-half bath could accommodate four people, whether that took into account the two caretakers and their bedroom is uncertain. Especially since the listing began in the singular: "Romantic room … near the beach" and unequivocally stated, "A total of 4 people can sleep here comfortably."

Romantic room. Not rooms. A total of four people …

Our hosts then told us we would be joined the next day by other guests and their dog. Wouldn't that be nice?

"If you had told us that earlier, we would have reconsidered …" was all I could muster, as we continued to take stock of the accommodations.

Our bedroom was at the front of the house, directly facing the trains. Mismatched furniture – a small "matrimonial" size bed with a well-worn mattress, throw pillows that felt as though they were filled with rice, two totally incompatible nightstands (one with a tiny lamp sold at most Chinese markets for ten euros), a bookcase, a round table with two chairs in front of the window – could all trace their ancestry to rummage sales or second-hand stores. Neither of the two bath towels on the bed compared to the ones we had bought at thrift shops in the USA for use as packing materials, and later used for the dogs.

An eclectic mix done well can be artistic and even elegant: "shabby chic." Chic? This place was plain shabby.

If you're renting this room out to a steady stream of

people, how about investing twenty euros on a clothing rack, instead of the over-the-door hanger with five hooks? Isn't that where bathrobes and towels hang? What about a bureau or chest-of-drawers? Where do people put their other stuff—underwear, socks, bathing gear, bathroom necessities, and collaterals? For that matter, where was a garbage can?

Nowhere near the bedroom, both bathrooms were way down the hall, beyond the kitchen. Add the full one (with shower and tub) and the half bath next door with only a sink and a WC, and you'd have one full and proper working bathroom. Depending on the time of day or night. Painted, one toilet was taped shut; the plastic toilet seat cover on the other wasn't attached; so, using it was awkward. The sink's faucets were outdated: scalding hot water came out of one spigot, cold from the other, yielding no comfortable temperature without filling the sink.

Not that it mattered. We had no hot water (in either bathroom) that night. Nor were our hosts around to help us deal with it.

The bathroom was missing a bath mat, an anti-slid mat, and a garbage can. The tub was lined with someone else's bottles of shampoo and conditioner–more than a dozen of them! Two glass shelves near the sink were full of creams and cosmetics, powders and perfumes. There was no space for anything of the guests, so we schlepped our toiletries back to the bedroom.

Settling down to sleep that night, we were thankful the trains, by then, had stopped. (Two did pass in the middle of the night: at 2:00 and 4:00 AM, but didn't honor us with their horns.) Sleepless noises were constant, however, courtesy of the beach and its breezes: the front gate and shutters banged open and shut … again and again and again.

Itching to bite, one or more mosquitoes whined in my ears throughout the night. I slapped my face but missed the bugger.

The next morning, I went quietly to the kitchen.

Sometime during the night or early that morning, someone had left a package of cheese open on a plate with a knife, a half-empty glass and coffee cup next to it. Flies weren't fickle as they feasted.

Russ saw the upset look on my face when I came back to our room. "Let's pack," he implored. "We're going back home!"

Following a hurried and harried breakfast at a nearby café, we hustled ourselves and the dogs out of there and headed back home.

Spending lazy time in Lousa and visiting nearby points of interest, we relaxed and tinkered together.

Merriam-Webster calls that a "staycation."

Language Lesson: A Portuguese Primer

The communications professor in me inherently wants to know about a language and understand what makes it tick.

Perhaps that's why Portuguese has been so frustrating to me ...

Peering through the peephole of Spanish, I try to unload the mysteries of how the Portuguese language works—and why.

But my Spanish causes obstacles, hurdles, and stumbling blocks. People constantly remind me that I'm thinking – and talking – in Spanish, not Portuguese.

"Fala português ... não espanhol!" they admonish and encourage me.

Intent at understanding the psychology behind the language, the rules governing its syntax, I've embarked on an ambitious project to analyze Portuguese, at least as the language relates to the Spanish I'm fluent in, and arrived at a number of "Eureka!" findings in the process.

Grab a pen and paper. It's time to take notes ...

Some rules hold true rather regularly between Portuguese and Spanish. For instance:
• An "n" in Spanish is usually an "m" in Portuguese, while the Spanish "ie" is simply an "e" in Portuguese. Examples: una/uma ... con/com ... en/em ... abierto/aberto ... diez/dez ... sin/sem ... tiene/tem ... bien/bem ... también/também ... alguien/alguem;
• That "ny" sound (as in "canyon") signaled by a tilde over the "n" (ñ) in Spanish is much the same in Portuguese, with words having "nh" letters: viño/vinho ... señora/senhora ... español/espanhol ... baño/banho ... leña/lenha. Although also used in Portuguese – most frequently over the letter "a" (ã) – the tilde produces an entirely different (nasal) sound: João ... cartão ... educação ... manhã ... não;
• The "ue" diphthong in Spanish becomes an "o" in Portuguese: luego/logo ... puerta/porta ... puede/pode ... fuego/fogo ... fuerza/força ... escuela/escola ...

111

cuenta/conta ... suerte/sorte ... juega/joga. Similarly, "ie" in Spanish is just "e" in Portuguese: siempre/sempre ... tiempo/tempo ... tiempo/tempo ... invierno/inverno ... fiesta/festa;

• "O" in Spanish is often "ou" in Portuguese: poco/pouco ... otro/outro, while the Spanish "l" often becomes an "r" in Portuguese: plato/prato ... placer/prazer ... plaza/praça;

• "U" in Spanish can become "ui" in Portuguese: mucho/muito ... at other times, instead, it becomes an "o": gusto/gosto ... punto/ponto;

• The double "ll" in Spanish often translates to "ch" in Portuguese: llave/chave ... llama/chama ... lluvia/chuvia ... llegando/chegando;

• Words beginning with "h" in Spanish often switch to an "f" in Portuguese: horno/forno ... hacer/fazer ... hablar/falar ... hijo/filho ... harina/farinha ... fugir/huir ... ... harto/farto;

• When you see a word with a "çao" suffix in Portuguese, it probably ends in "ión" in Spanish: relação/relación ... informação/información ... edição/edición ... habitação/habitación.

Confused?

Wait, the questions keep coming ... and we haven't yet touched upon sentence structure and tense:

Usually, it's "bom dia, boa tarde, boa noite" in Portuguese, but "buenos días, buenas tardes, buenas noches" in Spanish. Why are the day's divisions plural in Spanish but singular in Portuguese? At least for alliteration, if not mnemonic's sake, it should be the other way around!

Curiously, while one would say "No estoy seguro" (I'm not sure) in Spanish, proper Portuguese dictates saying "Não tenho certeza" (I don't have certainty). Yet one "has" (not "is") hot or cold in Spanish (Tengo calor; Tengo frío), while in Portuguese – as in English – you "are" hot or cold (Estou quente; Estou com frío).

Go figure ...

Thankfully, many words are identical in both

languages: "casa," "porque," "tal|vez," "médico," "viajar," "comprar," "poder," "vida" … and even "de nada," to say "you're welcome." So, how come cats are cats – "gatos" – in both languages, while a dog is "perro" in Spanish but "cão" in Portuguese? And, why do we give thanks with "gracias" in Spanish, but "obrigado," every foreigner's favorite word in Portuguese?

Pronunciation and accents are other matters entirely, as Portugal uses almost every accent mark in existence—and then some! How can anyone other than a native enunciate clearly the subtle differences between "pais" (parents), "país" (country), and "pães" (breads), when there's also "paz" (peace), "pás" (shovels), "pois" (because), "pôs" (put), "põES" (put), "pós" (dust), perhaps even more?

Still, Portuguese pronunciation follows much simpler rules than English. If you see it written, saying it correctly follows a standard set of rules. It may be hard to twist the tongue to produce that sound, but it isn't hard to know what sound you should be producing.

There is no doubt whatsoever of the correct pronunciation of any of the words above, and no linguists would argue over their correct pronunciation (regional accents aside). No argument, either, as how to pronounce "tomate" in Portuguese. Few are exceptions to the rules.

Now try the English language: Tomato (You say to-MAY-to, I say to-MAH-to). Why is Kansas so different from Arkansas? And why is "ough" pronounced so differently depending on whether it appears in enough, cough, drought, furlough, thought, through, borough? English has few rules and lots of exceptions.

"Drives a non-native crazy!" laments a Portuguese friend.

Then, again, here's where turnabout between the Portuguese and the Spanish isn't necessarily fair: Many – if not most – Portuguese people understand spoken Spanish. Spanish people, however, have a hard time understanding Portuguese orally.

Perhaps that's deliberate and explains why the

113

Portuguese language is so complicated? Maybe it's an act of protectionism by Portugal against its bigger neighbor to the east and erstwhile bully.

Navigating the same linguistic waters, Spain and I are in the same boat!

Benjamin Franklin & Daniel Defoe

"Our new Constitution is now established, and has an appearance that promises permanency; but in this world nothing can be said to be certain, except death and taxes," wrote Benjamin Franklin in 1789.

There's truth and (good) reason for this:

Trying to get a handle on taxes can be the death toll for many of us.

If dealing with taxes in one country is maddening, just wait until you're responsible for reconciling them between two!

USA citizens must file annual income tax statements with the IRS.

We also pay taxes here in Portugal and Spain. Plenty of them, many going by different names: taxes, fees, duties, levies, assessments, etc. Yet for expats living in Portugal, especially, there's good news and bad.

If you can understand how it works.

I don't. Do you?

(Hopefully, someone can clarify and explain it to the rest of us.)

The good news is related to Portugal's "Non-Habitual Residency (NHR) Status" which, supposedly, gives Portugal tax residents an opportunity to receive qualifying income tax-free both in Portugal and the country that's the source of their income.

NHR is a special Portuguese rule that eliminates taxation (exemption) or allows a reduced flat tax rate of 20%. According to NHR guidelines, as long as the source country of your income has the power to tax it (regardless of whether the tax is actually applied), Portugal won't.

As I write this, Portugal has double taxation treaties with 79 other countries that eliminate double taxation. International rules decide which country has the right to tax a given type of income.

If you're a Portugal tax resident with a foreign pension or dividend, the tax treaties often say that such types of income are taxed in the country of residence (Portugal has the right to the tax). Yet, if you're an NHR, Portugal applies an exemption (you pay zero tax on this income).

Not an NHR? Normal Portuguese tax rates apply.

Theoretically, NHR makes Portugal a tax-free jurisdiction for individuals receiving pensions, dividends, royalties, and interest income. Those involved in certain artistic, scientific, or technical activities also benefit from a lower tax rate of 20% for a period of ten years.

This means no double taxation for pension income or for employment and self-employment income earned abroad. Income not taxed under this agreement also includes royalties, pensions, capital gains, and investment or rental income.

(Capital gains from the sale of securities will be taxed, however, as will income sourced from a "blacklisted tax haven" that does not have a double tax treaty with Portugal.)

"The biggest draw of the program is the opportunity to reduce your income tax to zero," states Andrew Henderson in Nomad Capitalist's *How to Pay Zero Income Tax with Non-Habitual Residence in Portugal.*

Once Non-Habitual Resident Status has been granted, much foreign income of individuals with this status is exempt from Portugal taxation.

Anyone can apply for NHR status, as its only two requirements are (1) you must either be a citizen or a legal resident of Portugal; and (2) you cannot have been a tax resident in Portugal for at least five years prior to your application. Once you obtain Portuguese residence, you have until March 31st of the following year to apply for your NHR status.

There's more good tax news, too, I've heard:

United States citizens who live and work abroad may be able to exclude all or part of their foreign salary or earnings – even if they're "digital nomads" working online contractually for a U.S. company while living abroad – when filing their U.S. federal tax returns.

Taken together with the IRS Foreign Earned Income Exclusion (FEIE), NHR status in Portugal can reduce your income taxes significantly. Under Section 911 of the U.S. tax code, the FEIE increased from $102,100 in 2017 to $104,100 in 2018.

Bottom line here: how would this work in our case?

Here's what we've been told:

Between the two of us, we receive about $25,000 in retirement (Social Security + a small annuity) and other passive (interest) income, which will be mostly absorbed by the Married Couple Standard Deduction.

We also have $10,000 of earned income through my spouse's online work as an independent contractor for a company based in Wisconsin, USA, which we can run through the Foreign Earned Income Exemption. The only "tax" we'll pay is self-employment (FICA & Medicare) on that $10,000 (about 15%) ... but deductions we can take against it will lessen any "profit" (and self-employment tax) as low as possible. We may have to pay a small tax on that $1,000 of retirement/passive income not absorbed by the Standard Deduction, at a (2018) tax rate of 10%.

Then, we file with Portugal under our Non-Habitual Resident status.

# # # # #

Families in Portugal pay a lot in taxes, fees and charges ... so much that the country has achieved second place in terms of who pays the highest fraction of taxes in their electricity bills among EU reporting countries. Portugal comes up as the fourth country whose gas bill has a higher percentage of taxes reflected on its final costs.

(Germany, Spain, Italy, and Cyprus did not present any data.)

Eurostat released data that sheds light on these prices. Although the new data isn't complete – some countries declared their information to be confidential – Portugal is in the top three of the EU's highest electricity and gas prices. In 2017, only two countries had higher prices than Portugal: Belgium (28 cents per kilowatt-hour) and Denmark (26 cents per kilowatt-hour).

In Portugal, most families pay 23 cents per kilowatt-hour.

According to the Eurostat data, families in Portugal have the second highest tax burden in Europe (12 cents per kilowatt-hour). This means that 52.02% of the price is tax-related.

The European average stands at 28.94%, with Eurostat taking note that the variations on EU energy prices are reflective of different geopolitical situations, national energy mixes, network costs, and different climates.

Gas prices reflect the same issue for the Portuguese, as only Sweden (11 cents) and Ireland (0.096 cents) have a higher tax burden than Portugal (0.093 cents).

Taxes on products and services – such as electricity, gas, and the labor to dispense them – are familiar to Americans as "sales tax."

In the European Union, they're referred to as "VAT" (or "IVA"), an acronym for value-added tax. Although VAT is charged throughout the European Union, each member country is responsible for setting its own rates ... ranging from a low of 17% (Luxemburg) to a high of 27% (Hungary), with a minimum 15% standard rate required.

Compare Portugal's VAT (23%) with those of its neighboring countries competing for sales and services: Italy (22%), Spain (21%), France (20%), and Germany (19%). The difference in VAT between, say, Spain and Portugal (2%) may seem slight and insignificant, but certainly adds up!

From household goods and vehicles to cosmetics and clothing, and from the services of mechanics and trades people to doctors and dentists, that VAT can add up quickly.

VATs and IVAs aren't the only taxes we pay here. Annually, there are property taxes (relatively low both in Portugal and Spain) and a road tax (based on the assessed value of your vehicle). We paid Portugal a road tax of just about €140 for one year, and a property tax (plus a "late payment" penalty fine) of about €150. Given the superior conditions of the roads here in Portugal, we're happy to pay about U.S. $160 in road taxes – exclusive, of course, of the tolls we pay when driving along the country's spectacular motorways – and $175 for our property tax bill.

Other than tolls, there may not be specific "road taxes" in the USA, because they come out of the property taxes paid to your municipality.

"Things as certain as death and taxes, can be more firmly believed," penned Daniel Defoe in his 1726 book *The Political History of the Devil,* published well before Benjamin Franklin's infamous quote.

Until only recently, non-European citizens seeking citizenship (or residency) in Portugal had to provide proof of health care insurance conforming to certain criteria. Among them is what was known as "repatriation of remains." In other words, if you died here in Portugal, you had to guarantee that your mortal remains would be returned to your country of origin.

Not anymore. The law has been changed.

Now, whether by burial or cremation, with religious observations or not, one's final remains can be laid to rest here in Portugal.

That's a good thing.

Because, when my time comes calling, this is where I want to stay.

Liz Taylor Skies

It stopped raining today.

Finally?

Since we arrived in the Castelo Branco region of Portugal, it has rained every single day. And I understand that it has been raining here long before we got here.

Continuous, incessant, irritating rain. Sometimes drizzles, often downpours. Gray skies, winds, breezes, chills. All accompanied the daily rains whose spigot was more on than off.

Granted, given the dry and scorched lands so thirsty for nature's watering can – especially after the devastating fires that destroyed so many lives and so much property in Portugal, while draining Spain of its essential nourishment – the rains are to be welcomed. Even so, it lifts one's spirit to see the bright blue hues of the heavenly skies.

Apart from their topography and magnificent tourist attractions, nothing quite dazzles me as much in Portugal and Spain as the sheer brilliance of their skies.

Not every day, of course ...

But during the season — sometime between April and October — one cannot help but look up and be stunned by the spectacular vista that continues, undiluted and unabated, mesmerizing for stretches of time.

"Nice" days, even pretty ones, enjoin us in many places. The iron gray look of the U.S. Midwest ... the humid, murky vapors of the Southeast ... the biting cold brilliance of America's Northeast ... California's celestial coast ... all have their special, extraordinary moments — "thin places," as Marcus Borg would call them — when we're within touching distance of the divine.

Yet, to my eyes, everything else pales beneath the breathtaking expanse and azure purity of the Portuguese and Spanish skies.

They remind me of Elizabeth Taylor's eyes.

Rooftop Experiences

Infrequently do we think about the roofs atop of our buildings.

When purchasing a property, we may have their roofs inspected for leaks and other potential problems. We curse them for their wear and tear—and the rotten expense of replacing them periodically. Some of us mutter under our breath when we must climb a ladder to adorn them with timely ornamentation.

Roofs can make for great metaphors. But what about their sheer grit and beauty, the plumage of their composition?

In Portugal, like Spain, you can't help but notice the rooftops. Everywhere, they're as distinctive and colorful as a patchwork quilt sewn by the souls of seamstresses.

Unlike the pasty composite shingle, formidable slate, enduring metal, and flexible rubber roofs covering up most American properties, the weathered, multi-color brick and terracotta tiles atop homes of every stripe and size here in Iberia are characteristically appealing.

Indeed, they're integral to the landscape.

Perched on the steep, stepped grade of the countryside, we look down and across at the rooftops here from our vantage points on the balconies and terraces that are part and parcel of inter-connected buildings.

Roofs are their own crowning glory, telling tales out of school about the wear-and-tear they've experienced over the years. By the climate. Invading armies. And their genealogies.

Especially in areas dating back to Moorish times, these colorful wrappers can be windows into the souls of the people and their places. So, we feel for the feeble roofs remaining as vestiges of neighborhood "ruinas," reminding us of better times ... while waiting for these distressed properties to be purchased and reconstructed (top-down).

I'm reminded of what some refer to as "mountaintop experiences," those times and places when we feel truly connected to the universal, the integral, the almighty and eternal.

Have you ever climbed to the top of a mountain – or taken an elevator to the top floor of a skyscraper – and then looked down at the view below? Each offers an experience similar to peering at rooftops: Whether you are at the top a mountain or up on the roof, the world beyond looks very different.

Most of the time, life looms pretty large before me … filling my personal screen of attention.

But from the perspective of a roof here in a Portuguese town or a Spanish village, life seems smaller – not inconsequential – but smaller, simply part of what's going on in the world around us.

That's rather humbling, all things considered.

Shabbat Shalom/Assalamu Alaikum

It's just about six o'clock Friday afternoon in our village, and it appears that everyone is out in the street.

After a relatively mild and overcast day, the sun suddenly is blazing and burning off the sticky skies.

That is rather unusual here in Portugal, whose weather tends to feel more like a sauna than a steam bath during the summer season.

Little old ladies wearing their black widow's weeds move slowly, some clutching canes and others with walkers, heading towards the church. There are services tonight, not to be missed, although I'm told that church services are held every day here.

Seated on the wall which encircles the church, elderly men, solitary yet together, form a ring. They won't go inside. For them, it seems far safer to comment on their world, to cuss and complain about whatever, than to seek shelter or solace in the sanctuary.

Others, too, sit outside, in front of their houses, where it's cooler in the shadows cast by houses so closely facing theirs. Men use handkerchiefs or rags to wipe sweat from their brows, while the women – some of them, at least – fan themselves slowly with advertising circulars.

People are arriving home from work, with far too many vessels clogging and clotting the capillaries doing the work of major arteries on our tight little "main" street. They're impatient. Already, they've been held up by a tractor inching slowly, cobble by stone, down the road, as a shepherd and two dogs herd some sheep along the way. Then, there's a truck, blocking traffic, as it stops to unload groceries at the corner market.

Once the sheep and the truck and the tractor are out of the way, some drivers speed down the little road as if it's the Grand Prix, cell phones held up in one hand and cigarettes dangling from the other. Several mostly older men, with their wives as passengers, steadfastly refuse to press the accelerator and go any faster; why risk losing control, when they'll get there soon enough?

The smell of diesel fumes is intoxicating, anyway.

Ironically, unlike other places filled with anxious people squeezing too many vehicles into hold-your-breath spaces, nobody here honks a horn.

It's just not the way things are done here.

Just about now, the bus pulls up to the periphery of town, discharging a stream of people who'd left early this morning to work in the big city. They, too, crowd the street, trekking tiredly towards their homes.

But, first, they must stop for coffee.

Vehicles – cars, trucks, vans, tractors, and trailers – jockey for position to park three deep by coffee shops on streets where founders and planners hardly envisioned vehicles, when building such towns and villages. Maybe they didn't consider the implications of getting around in a place with three coffee shops, but not a single place to eat here in Lousa. So, vehicles are unattended momentarily, motors still running, while their occupants dash off for their evening caffeine fixes.

Meanwhile, the young folks – old enough to drive Mercedes-Benzes and BMWs, souped-up Fiats, Renaults, Citroens and Peugeots ... and roaring motos, especially – are eager to escape, to get out of town and go elsewhere. Somewhere. Anywhere but here.

Right about when things seem to be less hectic, disaster unexpectedly strikes: a truck too big for our street and being driven too fast, lops off the balcony of a nearby house. Concrete and balustrades topple heavily onto the street. Everything halts, as the momentary shock and silence quickly yield to a collective gasp that grips and takes hold in the village.

Suddenly, everyone is drawn, like a dragnet to the magnet, flies to a spider's net. People stand around, beers (not coffee) in hand, some puffing on cigarettes, opining on what happened.

No, it wasn't a "hit-and-run" ... the driver, head hung sheepishly, is there among the crowd, too, looking up to the torn-off terrace and around to the scrapes along the side of his truck and its missing mirror.

He shakes his head in amazement.

Somebody hands him a beer.

Slowly, as the sun sets, people disperse and quiet returns to our town, except behind the closed doors and fly curtains. It's cooler now. People are inside, watching television with the volume turned up too loud.

The church bells peal.

It's Friday night now in the village.

Tomorrow, the days of counting – segunda, terça, quarta, quinta, sexta – will be over for now and days with real names, Saturday and Sunday, will have begun.

Welcome to the weekend.

Bom fin de semana!

When the Saints Come Marching In

For heaven's sake, the Portuguese and Spaniards love their saints.

Or, perhaps it's their saints' days (many last longer than a day!), with all the festivities and closures, that they really appreciate?

As two of the most Catholic of countries, religious holidays are bountiful in both Spain and Portugal, where many of the same feast days and ferias are celebrated.

Holy Week ("Semana Santa"), the week before Easter starting on Palm Sunday, is recognized almost everywhere "Christian," as is Christmas. Both Portugal and Spain also pay tribute to the Eucharist through Corpus Christi, the "Body of Christ," with processions, prayers, bells, incense, singing, and church services.

Next to Jesus, most venerated is the Virgin Mary. Personally, we're reminded of that daily ... as the street we now live on is named Nossa Senhora Dos Altos Céus ("Our Lady of the Highest Heavens").

A four-day "Festa Nossa Senhora Dos Altos Céus" is the highlight of the year here in Lousa. In addition to all the religious homage featuring a procession along streets festooned with petals, marching band, icons held high on their floats, and people dressed in their finest, following along up town and down, a carnival-like atmosphere pervades the village with celebratory lights strung across streets, community meals, games of chance, carousing and partying. Then, it takes weeks for the community to clean up from all that revelry.

Portugal and Spain honor Mary on August 15th for the Assumption of Mary, and on December 8th for the Immaculate Conception.

Celebrated on the same day (November 1st) in Spain and Portugal, too, is All Saints Day: "Todos los Santos" in Spanish and "Dia de Todos os Santos" in Portuguese, a national holiday in the two countries.

From national to the local levels, every town, village,

and province in Portugal and Spain honors its own special saints, as well.

In Olvera, our town in southern Spain, it's Mary who's again praised. According to tradition, sometime around 1500, a shepherd found an abandoned virgin about two kilometers from Olvera and, there, the Olvereños built their hermitage, an object of worship and consolation to the townsfolk all these years. Back in 1715, Olvera suffered a severe famine due to a drought and prayed for the Virgin to intercede. And the rain came! Thanking our Lady of Los Remedios is a tradition now on the Monday of Quasimodo, toasting the Virgin with a special pastry known as the "Torta del Lunes de Quasimodo."

For the sheer quantity of saints having holidays, the prize goes to Portugal ... which has several saints honored across the country. Who hasn't heard of Fátima, Portugal's most famous Christian pilgrimage?

On May 13, 1917, three children saw a miraculous vision of the Virgin Mary in Fátima. Later that same year, other apparitions apparently were witnessed by large numbers of people at the site.

Nowadays, a candlelight procession through the town on May 12th leads to the sanctuary. The next day, crowds wave white handkerchiefs, as a statue of the Virgin is carried from the high altar to the Chapel of the Apparitions during the "Adeus" (farewell) procession the following day. A second pilgrimage is held in October.

The Portuguese celebrate November 11th as Saint Martin's Day, another national holiday, which honors a soldier who cut his cloak in half to help keep a beggar warm ... after which the sun came out to warm him. As a result, warm days at the beginning of November are called "St. Martin's Summer." The Portuguese celebrate this time – called "Magusto" – with bonfires and parties, lots of chestnuts and wine.

Respects are paid to John the Baptist (São João) in cities around the country on June 23-24.

With all due respect, however, nowhere are as many

saints recognized as in our little Lousa. Besides the principal holiday devoted to "Our Lady of the Highest Heavens," Lousa honors at least four favored saints.

In August 2018, Santa Luzia was exalted on the 4th and 5th with a procession and special exposition dedicated to her at our historical museum. Not two weeks later is a three-day (17-19) festival honoring Saint Sebastian (São Sebastião). Other saints officially recognized and revered in this small village with a population hovering at about 650 include Santa Bárbara and San Antonio (the latter is feted for three days in June with a sardine fest). The nearby town, Lardosa, sponsors its own four-day jubilee for Saint Anthony in August.

Yet, so enthralled is Lousa with its saints that Lousarte, our hometown cultural association, published a book entitled *Los Santos da Lousa e Outras Coisas,* available for purchase at the Lousarte museum.

Museums seem to be religion's realm today, albeit holy days, special events and occasions – births, weddings, funerals – notwithstanding.

Fewer people seem to be participating in church services on Sundays.

Lord knows – except for the elderly, mostly women at that – I hardly see people going into or coming out of churches when the bells toll.

There's an oft-told joke in Spain which, loosely translated, states that "A Spaniard will die defending the doors of his church. That doesn't mean he'll ever go in!"

I suspect the same may be more or less true today in Portugal, where, according to the 2011 Census, 81% of the population of Portugal is Catholic, although only about 19% attend Mass and take the sacraments regularly. A larger number wish to have their children baptized, be married in a church, and receive Last Rites.

Among the expats we know in both countries, quite a few consider themselves to be "spiritual," but organized and institutional "religion" tends to be avoided … with plenty of agnostics and atheists, instead.

THE BBB

Have you ever entertained the thought of retiring to some romantic place and opening a bed and breakfast there?

We have.

Nothing fancy, mind you; just a comfortable, offbeat place where weary workers or disheartened folks – single or couples – can relax and find some charm (or curiosities) and respite, off the beaten track.

For us, that means Portugal and southern Spain.

In these days of Airbnb, almost anyone can open a bed and breakfast. Anywhere. Even if you only have one "guest" bedroom to spare … or a sofa-sleeper in your living room!

Not long ago, we spent several days at a bed and breakfast outside a substantial suburb at the fringes of a major Iberian provincial capital. The chaps who own the place obviously love it and lavish cook-and-clean duties diligently on it daily. They've invested a lot of time, funds, and creativity in establishing an attractive B&B.

But it can be the little things – sometimes overlooked by people thinking they can create an idyllic bed and breakfast – that make all the difference between a memorable experience and one that won't be repeated anytime soon.

As many people are hoping to move away from the USA and open a B&B in Spain or Portugal, here are a few observations and considerations for building the better bed and breakfast (The BBB):

• Warmth—Beyond the comeliness and hospitality of a bed and breakfast is the mere matter of its comfort factor. As in temperature. Nobody enjoys staying in a bone-chilling room when it's raining and nasty cold outside. If heating is provided by a single source (i.e., the warm setting of an air conditioner), consider back-ups. Even a propane-powered (or electric) heater can turn an unpleasant environment into a more comfortable one. Similarly, an air conditioner is an essential cost of doing business when inviting people to stay during warmer times.

• Beds—Some people prefer to sleep au naturel. So, sleeping in a bed covered only by a nice duvet cover over a heavy blanket or comforter may be okay; but top (and bottom) sheets are better. After all, do you really want guests to wonder whose skin had caressed the comforter before they did?

• Breakfast—Juice, fruits, cereals and yogurt, eggs, tortillas, toast, an assortment of charcuterie, and coffee (or tea) are delicious. Tasty and fulfilling. The first day (and maybe the second). But lacking distinction in this all-too-important meal, day after day, can become tiresome and ritualistic. There's truth to the adage that, "variety is the spice of life."

• Lighting and Electrical—By all means, have enough. Some is good … more is better … too much is just enough! Many of us like to read in bed. A light – even a clip-one to the headboard – is essential. Who wants to get up just when we're ready to close our eyes and fall asleep, to turn off the overhead light(s), because there aren't any lamps on the nightstands on the side of the bed? Similarly, some of us travel with quite a few contrivances: computers, laptops, devices, irons, whatever. Outlets providing 110/220-AC/DC are essential!

• Slipping and Sliding—Already having suffered a broken a leg (and currently saddled with five pins around my ankle and a titanium rod in my shin), I have no desire whatsoever to repeat the experience. So, please – please! – consider your flooring … especially in the bathrooms. Shiny surfaces (aka "glazed" tiles) may look wonderful, but they can become sheets of ice when wet feet come in contact with them. Especially when trying to reach for that towel at the other end of the bathroom! How much safer and simpler are bath mats and a utilitarian hook close to the shower for hanging the towel.

• Hot H20—Honestly, is anything worse than running out of hot water when you're in the middle of taking a shower or about to begin shaving? Fortunately, today's technology can provide hot water, continuously, courtesy of relatively inexpensive, on-demand water heaters. If you're thinking of turning your place into a B&B, please be sure your guests don't get a cold shoulder without continuous running hot water.

• Computers—They may be called "laptops," but sitting in bed with a computer on your lap is awkward at best and doesn't work (at worst). The better bed and breakfasts provide a desk (and chair) where one can work online conveniently and comfortably.

If and when we open our own B&B, we promise that it will cater to these simple pleasures and necessities of life. Until then, there's always our guest quarters – a separate room with a private en suite – where friends and family are invited to stay here in Lousa.

Business or Pleasure?

Starting a business anywhere isn't easy ... or cost-efficient ... and we began to question the wisdom (and value) of opening a small "snack bar" outside of Castelo Branco that sells small-plated food: our Tapas Americanas.

In addition to rent, utilities, furnishings and/or fixtures, merchandise (or whatever you are selling), to be factored into one's business costs in Portugal we're told are:

• Legal Fees to start up the business. Good lawyers – and we have a great one! – are worth their time and fees. In addition to all the government "red tape," we understand that that the "council" of our municipality must approve the request to open a new business;

• Insurance (Health). With or without owning a business, to be granted long-term residency in Portugal, one must have, at minimum, specific health coverages. Our health insurance for the two of us costs about €150 per month;

• Insurance (Liability). The business will need coverage to protect itself and its owners (us!) against possible "injuries" suffered by customers and bystanders;

• A registered accountant is absolutely required. Add another €50-150 each month;

• Every employee, including yourself (as owner), must be paid at least the minimum wage. Currently, we're told that's €585 every month;

• Social Security Contributions. Each employee, including the owner, must contribute @ €184 per month to Portugal's Social Security system.

• Debit/Credit Card Fees. 4% of gross sales. Actually it's O.9% with BPI, Millennium and Novobanco; 0.75% with CGD and up to 1.5% with BIC. Minimum payment taken back by the bank is usually 0.05%

• Finanças and their 'connected' cash register(s).

• So, even before you open the door (assuming you have one) or invest in inventory or stock or ingredients for food to sell, one must cover monthly costs of at least €850!

If we sell our Tapas Americanas at the very reasonable

rate of €3 per plate (or dish), we would need to sell over 300 tapas per month just to meet our operating expenses ... not counting other overhead (utilities, etc.), salaries, and Social Security for each additional employee, and taxes.

Profits? LOL!

Driving School

Three months in the country, and I could barely put several words together into a sentence ... at least a sentence that makes some sense, even if not grammatically correct.

But I do read the posts in several online groups for people moving to Portugal and putting their affairs in order.

That's how I learned that, as legal residents of Portugal, we needed to exchange our USA driver licenses for Portuguese ones within 90 days of receiving our official residency permits ... or face taking driving lessons – and a test! – to be granted the right to continue driving here.

Before leaving the USA, we made sure to obtain official copies of our driving records (and history) from our state's department of motor vehicles. Easy enough to do online. We also had those documents apostilled from our state's department of state. A bit more complicated. But we had read and were alerted that EU countries, especially the more fastidious ones, can be sticklers for proper paper work embellished with fancy ribbons, seals, stamps, and signatures.

Our experience attempting to trade our American driver licenses for Portuguese ones, however, turned out to be a classic example of what can happen when operating systems collide rather than cooperate.

We had heard from other non-EU nationals (now legal residents here) that you can take care of everything needed to turn in your USA state's driver license and obtain a Portuguese one – including the required doctor's exam – at some driving schools. So, we used Google (.pt) to search for driving schools in our jurisdiction, Castelo Branco. We contacted each by email, explained our situation, and asked if we could fulfill all the requirements at their school(s).

After a week, only one had responded: "Come in and we can talk."

Friends who live in the lovely Alpedrinha area had

recently completed the driver license exchange process. "Just go to the driving school next to the Chinese restaurant in Fundão and they'll take care of it all," they advised us. "The medical exam isn't really an exam and, as long as you bring all the required documents, you'll be in and out within an hour."

Mission accomplished within an hour? Here in Portugal?

Not quite!

We contacted the Fundão driving school with the same email message sent to the others. Within an hour, however, we heard back: Yes, all could be accomplished there. Please call to make an appointment.

Google Translate opened on my computer, I telephoned and identified myself by name.

"Sim, sim …" the gentleman replied, followed quickly by a string of words I couldn't understand.

"Por favor, repita," I asked three times, until I understood that we could come either at 1:30 (13:30) or 6:00 (18:00) that same day. Wow! I managed to ask if we needed to bring anything with us … in addition to our USA driver licenses, our official driving records, and our residence cards. Did we need our passports?

"Nao, nao. É tudo."

Except that it wasn't.

It took half an hour and one motorway toll to get there on the A-23. We entered the storefront driving school and, immediately, the man behind the counter began talking to me, albeit in a monotone too fast for my meager comprehension. Without a computer and access to Google Translate, I tried my best to ask him to slow down and tried to explain that we couldn't follow what he was saying.

"Por favor: no falamos portugues. Você fala muito rápido. Nos não entendemos." Yeah, a bit of my Spanish slipped in.

He probably didn't get a word I was saying, as he didn't miss a beat in his rapid-fire statements and questions. But two elderly gentlemen, seated behind us against the window in old kitchen chairs, were just "hanging out" there and enjoying a chuckle over our goings-on. They nodded when we handed over our Wisconsin state driver licenses and Portugal residency cards for photocopying, continuing a commentary between themselves. But the man in charge kept up his monologue, rattling away at us in what sounded like one rapid, run-on sentence.

Smiling, one of the two men witnessing our exchange shrugged and, in faltering English, asked: "You understand he tells you? Castelo Branco. See doctor here. Papers in Castelo Branco." I smiled in return, remembering something we had learned in our first Portuguese class: When a word ends in the letter "o," it is pronounced as a "u." So, the jovial gent had spoken of our closest big city as "Cashtelu Brancu."

"If I understand correctly, what that man just said is that we could see the doctor here," I translated for Russ. "But the driving school can't give us our licenses. For that, we'll need to go to the IMT in Castelo Branco."

"Why?" Russ asked.

"I'm not sure. But I suspect it's because our residence cards show that we live in Lousa, Castelo Branco. This is Fundão, a different jurisdiction. I'm guessing that this school can do license exchanges for people who live in this municipality ... but our municipality is Castelo Branco, so we will need to take all the paperwork to the Instituto da Mobilidad e dos Transportes (IMT) there to complete our license exchange."

It turns out that everyone has to go to the IMT to get their Portuguese driver licenses.

Russ rolled his eyes and was about to say or ask something, when the driving school manager interjected:

"O número utente?" he called for, holding out his hand.

"Que?" I responded, still not understanding. *"Que precisa?"* What do you need, I hoped that I'd asked him.

136

"Os números utentes!" he retorted.

I knew I had heard that word before ... but couldn't remember where, when, or why. Then, it came to me. Bingo! Our *números utentes* were the numbers assigned to us for health care in Portugal. We'd received them at the Centro de Saúde in Alcains, the regional health care center that oversaw our smaller one in Lousa.

"Tenha os números utentes?" he asked, this time more urgently.

I summoned every last bit of Portuguese I had learned or absorbed, and answered to the best of my ability: *"Sim! Tenhemos os números utentes. Fuimos al Centro de Saúde en Alcains para ver o médico e recibimos nossos números."*

Hopefully, I had explained that we, indeed, did have documented health care numbers, which we received when we went to see the doctor at our regional health care center in Alcains.

"E onde estão?" he countered.

"Em nossa casa na Lousa," I answered quite sheepishly.

Back and forth we went. Didn't we have the numbers written down? Why didn't we know them? How could we expect to see the doctor without our official health care numbers? We would have to go to the health care center's facility in Fundão and ask them to find our numbers from the national system via their computers.

Attempting to give us directions with words and hand motions, he kindly told one of his driving school instructors, a pleasant young man who had just arrived, to take us there ... and to bring us back with our health identification numbers.

Winding our way up, down, and across Fundão's streets, we arrived at its Centro de Saúde, where the young man explained to the receptionist that we needed her to look up our números utentes. We handed her our residency cards and waited.

But, no matter the criteria – our names, residence

numbers, fiscal numbers, dates when we thought we were assigned the numbers in Alcains – our números utentes couldn't be found. They just weren't in the system, the national database, we were told. I overheard the administrative assistant telling the young man to tell us that we would have to return to Alcains and have the problem resolved there.

Courteously, the young man drove us back to the driving school and explained to his boss what had happened (or didn't) and why. This time, I understood the guy when he told us we would need to: (1) Go to the Centro de Saúde in Alcains and deal with the matter of our health care numbers; (2) Return to the driving school, with our números utentes, to see the doctor for our medical exam; (3) Drive to the IMT in Castelo Branco with all our papers; and, there, (4) Exchange our USA for Portuguese driver licenses.

"Can't we just pay to see the doctor?" I asked before leaving the driving school. "Or, can't we go to a private doctor for the medical exams?"

Nope. Only "public" doctors – some public doctors – conduct the medical exam for a driver's license in Portugal.

We got in our car and headed back to Lousa. There was nothing more we could do then and there in Fundão. When we arrived home, we looked through a pile of papers and, sure enough, there were two documents issued by the Ministerio da Saúde, Região de Saúde Centro, Centro de Saúde Castelo Branco, Extensão UCSP Alcains.

Identified as "Documento de Identificaço Do Utente do SNS," guess what the first line contained …

You got it: our números utentes.

I have no idea why the health center in Fundão couldn't find our health numbers. Not that it really matters anymore. The next day, we had 4:00 PM (16:00) appointments to see the doctor at the Fundão driving school for our Portuguese driver license medical exams.

And what document will we carry in our wallets everywhere now?

That goes without saying!

I Could Be Wrong, But ...

I believe a bureaucrat at the Institute for Mobility and Transport (IMT) here – elsewhere known as the Department of Motor Vehicles – just did me a favor. An über one, at that!

DMVs anywhere aren't anyone's favorite government agency, but the bureaucracies residents must deal with here in Portugal – IMT (driver licenses and motor vehicles), Finanças (Taxes), SEF (Immigration), and EDP (the utility company), especially – have been attributed as being challenging > frustrating > irritating > next-to-impossible.

That's not been the case for us here in Castelo Branco. Staff at these offices have been considerate, cooperative, and extremely pleasant.

Anyway, here's the story:

We'd been very careful about observing all of Portugal's requirements — particularly for non-EU nationals seeking to reside here – in terms of documentation and deadlines. Especially regarding the IMT. This is a country that only recently changed its rules about transferring one's driver's license from your country of origin to a Portuguese one ... without adequately announcing the changes and spreading the word.

Formerly, new residents of specific non-EU nationalities had six months from the date they received official residency to trade in their existing licenses issued elsewhere for new ones from Portugal. The law now limits that time to just 90 days, with serious consequences if you miss that deadline: driving school lessons followed by written and driving tests dealing with laws, practices, competencies, and the mechanics of how vehicles operate.

To exchange an American driver's license for a Portuguese one, you must meet all of the "regular" requirements – a completed application form, proof of residency, your current driving license, passport, NIF, and a fee – along with an apostilled driving record from your last state of residence, plus a physician's certificate that you are fit to drive.

We provided everything required by the Instituto da Mobilidade e dos Transportes (IMT) and, within two weeks, would receive our official license cards in the mail. In the interim, since our USA driver licenses had to be surrendered, we were given paper documentation to certify our legality to drive here. Our new driver licenses arrived in the mail and everything looked fine, even those horrible digital "mug shots."

All was well, we assumed … until I tried to rent a car.

"I am sorry," the car rental agent apologized. "But I cannot rent you a car. You haven't been driving long enough—only since last year."

What? I'd obtained my driver's license on my 17th birthday. At 69, I had now driven continuously for more than 50 years … with licenses from New York, Maryland, Virginia, Florida, and Wisconsin!

"Please forgive me," I responded. "But I don't understand."

The amiable chap pointed to a line on the rear side of my new driver license, which indicated that my license was first issued in 2017.

"How is that possible?" I asked.

He shrugged off the mistake and suggested I take it up with the IMT.

Someone at IMT had erred when entering into the computer all the information that I had presented.

Fortunately, I had retained a copy of my official Wisconsin driving record in PDF format and peered at it on my computer screen before printing it out. There it was, in black and white: I began driving in Wisconsin on March 9, 2008.

Maybe not 50 years of driving experience, but certainly at least ten!

I would need to revisit IMT to point out the error and ask for my license to be corrected. And, while there, I could also ask about renewing my driver license before

141

March 9, the day before my 70th birthday, when Portugal required new evidence of my fitness to continue driving.

Older drivers in Portugal need to undergo medical and psychological examinations when renewing their driver licenses at ages 50, 60, 65, and 70 ... drivers older than 70 are subject to a revalidation test.

My doctor told me not to worry: there was no need for him to provide the medical certification until January, just two months before my 70th birthday. But I was concerned; I wanted IMT confirmation of that.

By law, one's Portuguese driving license expires at 70 years of age; so, when you reach 70, you need to renew it if you want to continue driving. You then need to renew it every two years. Renewal can be done up to six months prior to the license expiring.

I took a Portuguese friend with me to speak on my behalf.

The lady who waited on us was flustered but friendly. While I had feared that the copy of my Wisconsin driving license showing the date I began driving there wouldn't be accepted because it didn't have an apostille (my only apostilled copy was turned in, along with my license, during my initial visit to the IMT). But it wasn't a problem.

The only problem was the printer, which refused to cooperate.

Spending half an hour checking for paper jams, removing and shaking the laser cartridge a number of times, turning the machine off and on again, my IMT representative was getting impatient. A co-worker tried to help, going through the same motions. The office manager was summoned. He, too, couldn't get the printer to work; but he called for a replacement ... which arrived within half an hour.

Meanwhile, my Portuguese-speaking friend explained my concerns about renewing my license within the required time frame to the IMT lady. She looked at the expiration date – March 9, 2019 – and did some mental

142

calculations: No problem, she said. We were within the six-month window and she could renew my license, on the spot, without me having to return to IMT later. And, based on the documents I'd already supplied, she'd renew it now for two years without any new certifications—medical or otherwise.

It's easy to groan and bemoan the system.

Likewise, we need to give credit where, when, and to whom due.

Portugal & Spain: Two Sides of the Coin

"Which is better: Spain or Portugal?"
"Which do you prefer: Portugal or Spain?"
"How does Spain compare with Portugal?"
"Am I better off in Portugal or Spain?"
People often direct questions like these to us.

There are no simple answers, as they depend on *where* in Spain vs. Portugal, *which* preferences (climate, food, location), and *how* is one better off (health care, cost of living, shopping and dining, etc.).

I can only speak from our own experiences and of our personal preferences. But, ultimately, it boils down to one's particular taste(s).

Ten years ago, we purchased a small holiday home in one of the "pueblos blancos" of Andalucía in southern Spain ... just about where the provinces of Malaga, Sevilla, and Cadiz intersect. "Vacation bolt" was a good term for it, as the words implied our pace and its purpose.

Once each year, we engaged caregivers and caretakers to pet-sit and oversee our home in the USA, while we rushed off for ten days (then two or three weeks, and finally a month) in Olvera, Spain.

In November 2016, we decided to move to the Iberia peninsula. Not just to our Spanish vacation bolt, but to Portugal as well.

As of March 2018, Portugal became our primary residence, while our little getaway in Spain was now our home away from home. For a variety of reasons – all peripheral to this piece – we were grateful that we could retire and share our lives with two such special countries.

We're now spending about three-quarters of our time in Portugal and one-fourth in Spain—the months of May and October, along with other times when we feel the urge to pick up and go.

Along with many similarities, we've noticed some differences, too, between the two countries, as well as the character of Portuguese people and Spanish.

To begin with, the language.

Spanish always has been my second language, but it's a stumbling block in terms of Portuguese. The languages bear enough resemblance that I can understand about 75% of the words in Portuguese. When written. Spoken, however, all bets are off.

Language is a reflection of a people and their culture, and so it is with Spanish and Portuguese. In some ways, Spanish is an intricately more complex language to learn, while – despite its discrepancies between written letters and spoken sounds – fundamentally, Portuguese can be friendlier and simpler to master.

And the people?

To an outsider, the Spanish appear to be a bit more bon vivants and "salidos" (extroverted) than their introspective Portuguese neighbors, who often display a melancholy soulfulness known as "saudade."

Think of the Portuguese fado and the Spanish flamenco.

In these contrasts and comparisons, please remember that: (1) They're based on our personal opinion(s) and observations; and (2) We're referring to relatively small towns and villages in both countries, not the major municipalities like Lisbon or Madrid, Porto or Barcelona.

The land and the climate of both countries' interiors are quite similar – blazing hot in summers, rainy and rather chilly in winters – though the ubiquitous churches found on their streets, squares, and plazas are different: Church buildings in Spanish towns and villages tend to differ (somewhat) one from another, while Portuguese churches look more alike, variations on the same theme and a standard blueprint.

Spain seems much louder, more boisterous and insistent. From the timber and pitch of people's voices when talking, to the incessant hands on the horns of their vehicles, the decibel level is much higher in Spain than in Portugal.

People in Portugal will pause and wait patiently (to a

point, at least), while cars and trucks load and unload, blocking their paths, or when drivers say their good-byes to passengers and stop to greet pedestrians passing by. Not so in Spain, where folks are in more of a hurry and you'd better keep moving or you'll quickly suffer the blare of punishing horns. Worse are the vendors – breads, gas canisters, fruits and fish – who clamor for attention by blasting their shrill horns in steady staccato bleats while traversing the steep but narrow streets. With each and every stop, their wares are shouted for all to hear.

What about the cost of living?

Honestly, except for property and income taxes (Portugal's are much lower), it's easier to make ends meet on a budget in Spain.

Much of that, undoubtedly, is due to the sales tax (IVA): 21% in Spain vs. 23% in Portugal.

A typical shopping cart at the supermarket – groceries, cleaning supplies, paper goods, cosmetics, etc. – runs about 10€ more in Portugal than Spain. Gasoline in Spain currently hovers around ten cents more per liter, while the best deals in Portugal are found at the industrial zones. Filling the tank quickly adds up. Similarly, propane canisters cost €15.50 in Spain vs. €25.50 in Portugal. Electricity, appliances, furniture, textiles, and lots of other goods are far cheaper in Spain than Portugal, too.

Finally, the food:

In a nutshell, we find the food to be better with lots more for the money in Spain than in Portugal. That's because of the tapas. There aren't many places where one can enjoy enough epicurean delights to satisfy any hunger (usually including a basket of fresh bread and a plate of peanuts or olives) for just two to three euros. Add another euro for a glass of wine or a beer; both are cheaper than water or soft drinks in Portugal and Spain.

But Spain doesn't come close to Portugal for delicacies and desserts. When I die, I hope heaven (or the alternative) turns out to be a Portuguese pastelaria!

How people deal with their disposables is another study

in contrasts. While both Spain and Portugal provide readily accessible garbage bins for people to dispose of their trash, trash collection occurs daily – even on weekends ... Sundays, included! – in Spain. Instead, it's picked up from the bins about three times each week in Portugal. One's trash is treated more personally in Spain, too, where people hook and hang their bags like laundry on a line – on gates and grills, doors and windows – for pick up right by their houses.

Because of history and geopolitical reasons, some Portuguese have an attitude toward their neighbors in Spain.

And vice-versa.

Thankfully, we are Americans who appreciate the virtues and values of both countries!

Climate Change

"The rain in Spain stays mainly in the plain."

Don't you believe it, regardless of what Eliza Doolittle may have drilled into your head in *My Fair Lady*.

Lots of rain in Spain – as in Portugal – falls all over the place.

Especially, wherever we happen to be.

For those new to the Iberia peninsula, the rain takes some getting used to (as does the sun). Because of their grit and wherewithal, they're quite different forces from what we'd experienced in the USA.

We've lived in places from Northeast Wisconsin (Sturgeon Bay-Door County) to the First Coast of Southeast Florida (Jacksonville), and have dealt with nasty weather—both bitterly cold and infernally hot.

But, it's different here in Spain and Portugal.

We were accustomed to rainy days throughout the year, regardless of the season, in the USA. Spring, summer, fall, and winter … each had periods of rain awash with sunny skies. Here, however, on the pond's eastern front, there's a rainy "season" and a blazingly hot one.

Both are extreme and extensive.

Day after day, for weeks on end, we'll see little or no sign of rain during the sunny season in Spain and Portugal. Contrarily, during their time, we have dismal gray skies and lingering rain that never seems to end.

I respect the rain, especially in places where we live off the land's produce. And who doesn't? So, I'm not really complaining. But, hey, if we can't groan about the weather, what else can't we gripe about?

The rain, itself, is of a different sort; it has its own shelf life here.

Rain cycles incessantly from cold, bone-chilling downpours to storms, showers, and/or drizzles … then, repeat: again and again and again. Even without extended exposure to it, you feel as if pneumonia is more than presumed. Duvet-diving weather, it requires an air conditioner inverter turned on to its "heat" settings and an electric blanket (upper or lower) plugged into service.

Lower? Yep: in Portugal, our favorite electrodomésticos stores sell electric blankets that wrap around the mattress beneath us, instead of heating the top blanket which we pull over ourselves.

The weather is fickle and you never know when it will spike ten degrees or drop twenty during a 24-hour period. So, be sure to pack accordingly. Plan to layer. One day I wear a T-shirt; the next a long-sleeve shirt; the day after that, a T-shirt underneath a long-sleeve shirt; and, following that, a sweater over a long sleeve shirt and T-shirt.

Summers are hot, scorchingly so. We're talking about temperatures rising to and then hovering in the high 90s (F)/40s (C) range … in the shade (if you can find any) … for weeks, even months, on end.

That's why we have siestas/sestas here.

Not (just) to relax, but to escape the ravages of the weather.

We don't have central heating or air conditioning in our village homes and town houses. Fireplaces and wood burners, gas or electric heaters, keep us warm, room by room. Venture away from climate-controlled spaces, however, and put your hand on the walls. They're wet … dripping cold-hearted sweat!

And, woe is me if the flame on our gas-fired water heater should go out because of the rain or wind that often accompanies this intoxicated weather. Especially during winter's drafts.

We just replaced old, single pane glass, metal-framed windows and bedroom balcony doors with new ones of textured duplex glass, framed by vinyl and aluminum. Next on our Spanish bucket list will be to buy and install a new water heater which, currently, is strategically located on the terrace right outside our bathroom.

Speaking of buckets, don't forget to put one or more "draft dodgers" on the list for those exterior doors under which creep currents of air (hot and cold). Houses in Portuguese villages and Spanish towns usually are built out of concrete and cement, without insulation, and at rather odd angles. Rare is the door that meets the ground squarely.

We'll need a new roof, too. Several of the original, irreplaceable tiles on ours are cracked (causing leakage) ... and the old wormwood beams supporting the heavily tiled roof are virtually hollow, eaten through by worms over the years.

Mother Nature has her issues here, even as she did back in the States. Hurricanes. Wildfires. Floods. Earthquakes. They're all increasing in frequency and intensity, looming larger and lasting longer.

During our recent month (October) in Spain, Portugal was smacked by a rare Atlantic hurricane – the most powerful to hit the country since 1842 – which made landfall near Lisbon and then took a beeline directly to our home in Castelo Branco, close to the Spanish border.

Spain has been deluged by flooding that turns creeks into mighty rivers, carrying away heavy vehicles and causing landslides along the way. Areas of seismic activity have produced jolts of earthquakes too close for comfort to our little place in the sun.

In Portugal, we hadn't yet recovered from the encroaching forest fires, when 800 people — Portuguese activists, surfers, fishers, youths and supporters from around the world — came together on August 4 at Cova do Vapor beach outside Lisbon, where the Tagus River meets the Atlantic, to protest the country's plans for offshore drilling and inland fracking.

Still, there's something quaint and comforting about dealing with the weather in old-fashioned ways: locals providing for neighbors in any ways possible, fanning themselves with papers, and moving to the lower levels of their homes (where it's cooler) in the heat. Lighting fires and bundling up to keep warm in the winter. Shrugging off the weather by remembering that, after all, tomorrow is another day.

Soon enough, those spectacular azure skies will appear!

Then, Again. But Better!

There's just so much you can do with 55m2 (not even 600-square-feet), when one-third of the space is taken up by a bathroom and terrace. When a double/full-size ("matrimonial") bed occupies the majority of the bedroom level. When the only other floor (ground level) measures just about 10 X 15 (15m2 at most) ... and comprises our entry and reception area, an office, kitchen, eating space, and living room.

Quite the creative challenge to reclaim that three-story townhouse and return it to a home that's functional, yet comfortable and cozy.

But such was our task when we purchased a little vacation bolt in one of the "pueblos blancos" dotting Andalucía (southern Spain) about ten years ago ... sold it to a British chap when "la crisis" decreased its value by at least 50% ... and then bought it back from him this year, when he decided that he preferred life on the coast.

The town is Olvera, a hamlet with a population of about 10,000 (including a great assortment of expats from more than a dozen countries), with spectacular vistas and lots of steep streets. Most of these streets would be called "alleys" elsewhere; but many do allow for two-way traffic, as well as parking on one side of the street (which often rotates on a monthly basis).

Trying to move vehicles through this obstacle course of pedestrians and pets competing with cars and trucks for limited space results in dings and scratches, bangs and bumps, which the natives affectionately refer to as "Olvera Kisses."

It also makes it difficult to transport, load, and unload both passengers and cargo – groceries, furniture, supplies – since, every time you stop, the street backs up and the horns start blaring. Redecorating can be trying when one needs to remove old stuff and bring in the new.

That's what faced us as we made the six-hour drive from Portugal in a van loaded with two adult men, three pet dogs, and household items ranging from towels and linens to pots and pans ... pet food, pet toys, and pet beds for three very spoiled Schnauzers ... objets d'art, kitchen gadgets, tools, and other assorted essentials.

In the years since we'd sold the place, little had changed: most of the furniture, appliances, artwork, dishes and glasses that we'd originally put in place were still there – and then some – even if their current placement and arrangement didn't agree with our personal tastes.

We emptied bureau drawers filled with odds and ends of papers and outdated manuals; we removed posters taped to the walls; we sorted through what had once been complete sets of dinnerware, flatware, and glasses; we moved furniture to discover hidden art treasures (along with other debris); we donated an oversize recliner chair to charity; we took out numerous bags of rubbish for pick up by the bin men, while a 10-year-old mattress slept on by who knows how many people went down to the dump.

Then the "real" work began: replacing old, single pane windows and doors with heavy metal frames that took up valuable space by opening in rather than sliding side-to-side on tracks with bonus fly screens; painting the concrete walls which had been damaged by replacing the windows and doors (as well as the toll taken by years of "damp" and moisture that build up when fresh air doesn't circulate in unventilated spaces during the wet weather); dealing with an obsolete, overflowing water tank on our roof and a fickle water heater on the terrace; rearranging the furniture to better suit its purposes; and shopping, shopping, and more shopping for all the stuff that we needed (and things that we didn't need but wanted).

We made what had been ours (then) ours, again.

But better!

6 Rms Riv Vu?

People are moving to Spain and Portugal ... and they're looking for property, whether to buy or to rent.

If you're planning to relocate abroad, you'll need a place to live. That's not just common sense, but a legal immigration requirement: When applying for an EU visa and/or residency permit, expect to document your domicile in the country either with a deed showing that you own a property ... or a bona fide (minimum) six-month rental lease.

Increasingly, consulates and immigration authorities are casting wary eyes on the ubiquitous Airbnbs, making it more difficult to be granted a visa if you're planning to stay at these temporary lodgings lucrative for entrepreneurs and home owners alike.

Unless you know someone with boots on the ground, speak the language well enough to be treated like a local, or are lucky by happenchance to be in the right place at the right time, finding an acceptable place to live means turning to "property agents" (real estate agents and Realtors® in the USA) to help and guide you.

Boa sorte!

The property representation enterprise differs from country to country within the European Union, and is altogether different from what we have experienced back in the States.

Beginning online ... where most people start their property searches.

"I viewed lots of properties ... one was right next door, as the agents didn't have a key for the one I'd asked to see! Room sizes are rarely mentioned. And quite often there is no photo of the front of house!" recalls one relatively new resident who spent hours online looking at properties listed by multiple agencies. "The price can vary if it's with more than one agent. I viewed a place that had four different prices, with €25,000 between the lowest and highest!"

Here's some (unsolicited) advice to property agents

that's important for readers to consider, too, in their property search:

The property agent's job is to help you find the best place for your needs and budget. Simply listing a property on a website and other property "portals" isn't enough to motivate us. When considering a property, whether for purchase or rental, there's lots of information we want and need—and we'll be looking for it, first, online.

So, property agents:

• Please be accurate and detailed in your listings: Don't tell me that a property has 4 BR + 2 BA in one place and then say it has 2 BR + 1 BA in another. Often, multiple agencies will list the same property … but with different (and, sometimes, conflicting) information. Whether the property is connected to municipal water and sewer mains (and/or has wells and a septic tank or field) ... if the water is heated by "bottled" gas, gas lines, or electricity ... the condition and construction of the windows, doors, and roof ... which appliances and what furniture shown in the pictures are included in the price ... all of this matters to us and makes a difference regarding those properties that interest us.

"Oddly enough, the written description is the last thing I read," admits a newcomer, posting online. "I could quote you 80% of the descriptions I've seen so far as every house is in a quiet village … a five-minute walk from cafés … has excellent sun exposure … and is accessible, offering fast and easy access to the main roads and highways."

The old "6 Rms Riv Vu" syndrome, huh?

Yet it's quite true: many properties in Portugal, especially, are located in quiet villages ... have a five-minute walk to cafés ... and offer quick access to the main roads. That's because much of the infrastructure here in Portugal is great, offering the charm and quaintness of small villages, along with easy access to larger cities.

• Pictures are worth thousands of words. The more (current) pictures posted of a property, the more (or less) attractive it will appear. Pictures of any land included with the property are nice, but – by and large – we'll want to see the inside of properties where we may live. Thirty-four pictures of the garden and local river beach with few photos of the rooms inside will cause most to move on or look elsewhere.

"I looked at so many places online with no interior pics," exclaimed one frustrated customer. "So, I just passed straight on to next!"

Yes, we'll be noticing those cracks in the walls, the missing tiles on the floors, the damp mold on the ceiling, the condition of the roof and its wood, cement, or metal beams. After all, shouldn't we?

• If one agency identifies a property as "T3" (a three-bedroom home) showing no internal pics, and the other says "T4 + 1" (four-bedroom home + one additional bedroom ... somewhere), yet only shows photos of two bedrooms, how many bedrooms does the house, in fact, have?

One of the property agents we know in Spain includes diagrams with each listing, showing the size and configuration of all rooms in the property. This is very helpful, as descriptions and pictures themselves don't tell the whole story. Frankly, I don't want a bathroom in my dining room ... or outside on the patio. This little "extra" provided by the property agency has been instrumental in its growth and success!

• People are especially interested in where a property is located.

"Why won't some agents tell you where a property is? Seems a really basic thing to me!" shares someone who's looked at quite a few places. "If you don't want to put a map location in the listing, please, just tell me where the house is. I want to see the surrounding area on the map. And if there's a fair bit of land, then a boundary plan is essential!"

• Present the property in its best possible light and, please, make it appear appealing.

Dirty dishes in the sink, messy bedrooms, and

mismatched furniture arranged helter-skelter tell us a lot about whether the previous owners took good care of the property ... and whether a property agent really is motivated to represent and sell that property.

• Some properties have been vacant and on the market for a long time. Please make sure that they are "decent" when you show them to us. We don't want to see dead bats or birds on the floor ... evidence of mice and rodents ... or run into spiders and cobwebs, dust bunnies, and other obstacles that cause us to leave quickly, run home, and bathe or shower immediately!

"I visited a house inhabited by a family with a toddler," recalls a friend. "There were so many cobwebs that would beat Halloween decorations, the main room was messy with dirty laundry all over the place, and a big bicycle stood in the living room. I was surprised how someone could sit on the couch, letting her toddler walk around in such a dirty place!"

Nonetheless, opinions differ about what we should expect in both properties and from their representatives in Iberia:

"I think there is a cultural difference and you are looking for something as an American in Portugal that the Portuguese don't care about," says Jeff. "Both of the apartments we rented in Lisbon had junk in photos. The first had a huge pile of construction material in one room and the other had a pile of ash on the kitchen counter. Nobody thinks anything about it and you just tell the landlord to make sure it's clean before you move in. I'm sure it's the same for homes being sold. It's a difference between the U.S. and Portugal, like expecting fresh sardines to be gutted before they are cooked."

To be sure, no properties built in Spain's smaller towns and Portugal's villages are "level," "square," or "plumb." Most of the properties have their own peculiar quirks, as there are few (if any) real building codes required ... especially in the smaller villages. With steps of different heights and widths, and slight little step-downs or -ups between rooms, mobility can be a major accommodation factor. Even those of us without wheelchairs have tripped, slipped, or bumped into something all-too-often. It's part of the "character" of these village properties.

• Before making an offer on a property, get a "survey" done on it.

Nobody should buy a property without a home inspection ... even in Spain and Portugal. You need to know about potential problems with the roof, water service, electric, and hiding inside the walls.

Although I've yet to see home inspectors, per se, promoting themselves as such, their evaluations and assessments, called "surveys," are available here. Ask online for recommendations and referrals.

• If we do respond to a listing on an agency's website or one of the property portals it uses, property agents should endeavor to reply to our inquiries as quickly as possible. Answer our questions and arrange for us to see the property. While "location, location, location" and its condition may be factors in determining a property's price, all too often, "time is of the essence" for us. Our time is limited when we've come, primarily, to find a property.

So, after we view a property, please get back to us quickly with answers to our questions, reassurances about our concerns, and any additional helpful information that you can provide.

"The real estate market in Portugal offers the luxurious, the good, the average, and the mediocre ... with prices adjusted to the condition of the property," asserts one local, "depending on what you are looking for, where you're looking, and your available budget."

That's why proper property representation is vital.

"I used to be an estate agent in the Netherlands," relates one property agent. "I can't get my head around the fact that the agents often don't get a monthly income, just commission, but they haven't figured out that improving their service will lead to more sales. If the only money you make is commission-based, you need to sell."

For Whom the Bells Toll

The rhythm of life in the villages of Portugal and Spain's small towns is measured more appropriately by "ding-dongs" than "tick-tocks."

That's because church bells – not timepieces sans striking mechanisms or apps on digital devices – effectively (and efficiently) call us to come and go, awake and sleep, to accommodate time … with chimes whose claims remain diligent reminders in the background of our lives.

After a lifetime living near the deafening roar of airport jets taking off and landing, the blaring alarms of late night and early morning trains approaching crossings closed by mechanical arms, and the deeply mournful bass horns of ships passing in the night harbor, we sought a simpler life with sounds that relax and reassure, rather than jolt or jar.

Our favored vision of an idyllic retirement was marked by two indelible images: meandering cobble stone streets for walks and wandering. And church bells nearby, easing our todays into tomorrows with yesterdays' bygones … periodicity to their perennial peals.

Peals before swine?

The church bells at our village's central plaza echo the pulse of the people, their ebb and flow, undertaking life's daily tasks and rituals.

They summon morning strollers and diesel drivers; elderly men that sit on the church walls to jawbone about this and that; women who rise and shine to stop and shop for necessities at the local market; youngsters going to or coming from school.

The bells ring four times right before each hour to alert us that the full hour count(down) is forthcoming. They toll once at 15 minutes after the hour, twice on the half hour, and thrice every 45 minutes past the hour. At sunrise and sunset, they peal serially: three times three. To alert the village of urgent news and "special events" – the beginning and end of Sunday services, the baptism of a new life, or a cadence for the dearly departed – the bells ring rapidly, continuously.

Minutes apart, earlier or later, bells of the other churches in our village momentarily repeat the offbeat chant.

Elsewhere, church bells play a major musical intermezzo at 7:30 and 18:30 each day, calling the faithful to prayer. Some swear that their village bells play Clementine, an American folk tune, albeit with medieval disco vibes.

It's said that, originally, the bells rang to let workers in the fields know they had a few minutes to begin work, break for lunch, and finish ... ringing a couple of minutes before the hour to let them know it was nearly time. And that there were different timbres so, when out on the land, you recognized which of the bells to listen for—yours.

In some places now, the bells don't ring between 22:00 and 5:00.

But not here in Lousa. They've become biorhythms, conditioning us to sleep through their nocturnal and diurnal tirades.

Based on a sermon by John Donne, *For Whom the Bell Tolls* is the title of Ernest Hemingway's 1940 novel about the 1930s Spanish Civil War. The phrase refers to church bells that are rung when a person dies.

Donne says that, because we are all part of mankind, any person's death is a loss to all: "Any man's death diminishes me because I am involved in mankind, and therefore never send to know for whom the bell tolls; it tolls for thee."

Hemingway suggests that we should not be curious as to for *whom* the bell is tolling—it's tolling for us all!

Ding-dong. Ding-dong. Ding-dong.

Living in Lousa

"If this property were located in Castelo Branco, not Lousa, it would be worth €100,000 more," the ReMax property agent told us. "Property buyers aren't looking here ... they want to live closer to the city."

There are plenty of places to choose from—including Coimbra's Lousã!

Technically, Portugal's mainland is divided into 18 districts (distritos) formerly referred to as provinces; 278 municipalities (concelhos); 159 cities (cidades); 533 towns (vilas); and 2,882 civil parishes (freguesias). Countless "unofficial" villages, like Lousa, add to these numbers.

Granted, our little village isn't the biggest, the best, or the prettiest.

Other places in Portugal have those honors. Lousa doesn't have the tourist attractions. It's not located in one of the more popular places. With 35.82 km² of area and 621 inhabitants (2011), its population density is 17.3 hab / km². And, apart from two cafés, it doesn't even have a snack bar ... let alone "shops," except for two competing caddy-corner grocery markets (we've yet to learn the history behind that) and a beauty salon open on Wednesdays and Saturdays.

Without fame or fortune, Lousa perfectly delimits the "it is what it is" syndrome: nothing more, nothing less. Perhaps that's why some people are keeping their distance? With few non-native English speakers, we're the only Americans in town.

Like so many little villages across Portugal, Lousa is an appendage, abolished in 2013 under administrative reform and added to the parish of Escalos de Cima. (Similarly, Escalos de Baixo took on the village of Mata.) Perhaps we in Lousa should derive some pleasure that, at least, we're annexed to the high "scales," not the low ones.

Part of the "L" triumvirate – Lousa, Lardosa, Louriçal – surrounding the A23 motorway, just south of the popular Fundão and Covilhã cities, Lousa's streets (which follow neither rhyme nor reason) are too narrow to cast shadows. Without a stop sign or traffic light anywhere in sight, motorists race across these roads with wild abandon ... or inch slowly but surely, as the tortoise to the hare. It's a miracle there haven't been accidents, as walkers wedge themselves against the walls of buildings and meandering dogs dodge the horseless carriages speeding their way.

Anchored by a standard blueprint church, the village plaza with its fresh water fountain next to the rectory is the trunk from which street stumps and stubs branch out in all directions. You'll find some truly grand homes here which, in their heyday, must have been primo properties for the privileged. Clustered around them are row houses of varying shapes and sizes. While pride of ownership is obvious in many of these homes, others have withered and weathered, generation after generation, inherited but hardly inhabited. Unlike USA townhouses, no two buildings are alike. There's no prevailing regularity or symmetry. Some have doors so improbably short that only the smallest of people can fit through them.

Cobble stone streets are simply engineered, higher in the middle mains and lower on the sides, enticing the gushing rain water to run off and disgorge into the sewers in front of our doors. The village's perimeter is ringed by large farms ("quintas"), land holdings, and the cemetery.

Lousa has a Day Center where our seniors congregate. We've got a Centro de Saúde, too, allowing residents to wait hours on Tuesdays to consult the doctor. A primary school epitomizes the one-room schoolhouse, where twenty or so youngsters (all told) learn their lessons. Our village sports several small parks and an arena of sorts, where children play and adults can compete.

People trudge to a sheltered bus stop at the village entrance and sit on concrete benches, waiting for transportation to and from the big city where they work and shop. Just down the street is our "junta" office, where the village's business is administered for a half hour or so on Tuesday and Thursday evenings.

Animals abound. Homeless dogs and cats roam the streets in search of morsels of food remaining on whatever's been thrown out for them. Sheep, too, pass through the streets twice daily, nudged from behind by a man driving a tractor; flanking their sides are two shepherd dogs. Meanwhile, geese, ducks, donkeys and burros, horses, roosters and chickens, and other assorted livestock all contribute to the cacophony.

Triaged throughout the village, trash bin trios are strategically sited. And a plethora of directional signs point the way to get elsewhere.

Some things truly are special here: Lousarte is the village association, a cultural center and "museum" showcasing Lousa's traditions and vast social heritage. Lousarte already has two sections, Traditional Dances of Lousa and a Theater, and has published a book about the village's saints (male and female). We also have the União Lousense, a recreation club where one can exercise with a trainer two nights each week.

In addition to holidays venerating its special saints, Lousa has popular celebrations that bring people together: a chestnut roast, communal tasting of the season's first wines, and sardine festivals (among others).

We've gotten to know the cast – including the village "characters" – and those who routinely stop for their morning coffees, departing the café hacking persistent smoker coughs ... and they've come to know us. A klatch of women who gather at our market to chew the fat enjoy our attempts to speak their language. Sadly, they smile and tutor us.

We're probably the first non-EU nationals who have chosen to settle here in Lousa. As human bodies biologically adjust and adapt to an infusion or a transplant, so, too, have the Lousenses accepted and accommodated us as part of their community. Initially, we may have been those two "strange Americans" who moved here, installed fly screens on our windows, walked our dogs on leashes and picked up after them ... but we've been adopted by the good people of this town and, now, we are treated as their very own personal Americans.

Despite the naysaying property agents, growth is occurring here in Lousa, as new buildings are constructed on the outskirts. Even we are purchasing a piece of property, land where the neighbors are quietest … on the R/do Cemetério. We'll learn to grow foodstuffs and, perhaps, will open a small shelter for the village's dogs and cats of the street.

Lousa, the overlooked stepchild and less likely half-brother or sister, has taught us to understand "Saudade," the uniquely Portuguese spirit of a nostalgic longing to be near again to something or someone distant … or to what has been loved, but then lost.

Saudade na Lousa.

It's the "love that remains" here, full of soul.

Day Care

No matter how small or fragmented the freguesia, there are always some signposts you'll see at the entrance to every Portuguese village and town – most Spanish ones, too – directing you to such important places as the local health care center, school(s), "mother" church, sports fields, and cemetery. Somewhere between them is a directional arrow pointing to the local "Centro de Dia."

It's a day care center … but for the elderly, not children.

Neither nursing homes, assisted living facilities, or convalescent care, these social service agencies offer long-term support to senior citizens and their families who aren't sent away to old age homes or residing in retirement communities.

Instead, they're staying in their homes—with supplemental help from their local senior centers, providing them care daytime and later, too.

In another world, I handled public relations and marketing for the Jefferson Area Board for the Aging – JABA – in Charlottesville, Virginia. Thanks to the vision and dedication of its long-time director, Gordon Walker, JABA was in the vanguard of the "ageing-in-place" movement for the elderly who needed some help, but wanted to continue living in their homes surrounded and comforted by the life they knew so well.

One of my first responsibilities was to help "brand" the nonprofit by developing a logo and slogan or motto that accurately reflected JABA's humanitarian mission and goals. Following a fruitless pursuit of using the letters J-A-B-A creatively to manipulate a catchphrase, we got back to basics and hit the nail squarely on its head:

"Live better. Longer."

After all, wasn't that JABA's purpose, what it all was about?

Portugal and Spain are ahead of America when it comes to caring for their elderly. In December 1996,

Lisbon's Directorate General for Social Action published a paper outlining the role and range of responsibilities a "Centro de Dia" would serve in its community.

The concept of the Day Center was to be, "a social response, providing a set of services that contribute to the maintenance of the elderly within a socio-family environment." Its objectives are three-fold: (1) providing services that satisfy basic needs; (2) facilitating psycho-social support; and (3) to avoid isolation, fostering interpersonal relationships between the elderly and other age groups.

In plain English?

The Day Center is intended to improve quality of life for the elderly and enable them to be maintained in their own home environment.

Like many European countries, Portugal (and Spain) faces a growing elderly population, which increases the pressure on both institutions and professionals to provide social and therapeutic care in the most cost-effective way possible.

"Integrated" care – Day Centers – emerged as a response to these challenges, ensuring uninterrupted care; improving access to and personal satisfaction with quality health care; and raising the efficiency and effectiveness of social and health systems ... all with the goal of patient empowerment.

Benefits of engaging with a Day Center include:
• Activities designed to stimulate, improve, or maintain the elderly's physical and intellectual capacities;
• Social, leisure time, and recreational pursuits—including day trips;
• Intergenerational workshops that advance the arts, caretaker skills, and manual dexterity;
• Meals, served on-site and delivered to homes;
• Transportation;
• Coordination and liaison with local health agencies;
• Personal hygiene and laundry services.

In addition, Day Centers can contribute to domestic support at home, as well as to provide temporary shelter.

Lisbon 1996's guiding directives call for a Day Center serving 30 clients to employ six staff members: a technical director, physical therapist, driver, cook, center and family associate, and an aide.

With ten employees – along with part-time visits from a doctor, social coordinator, nurse, physiotherapist, nutritionist, and a trainee – our Day Center in Lousa serves 47 elderly people: 24 on site at its facility and 23 more at their homes.

Darting around the village, delivering meals on wheels to homebound seniors unable to be at the center, vital and vibrant staff members bustle about, wheeling and dealing with their elderly charges.

Fees vary, according to the number of services and routine provided, and paid – for the most part – by Social Security, with small monthly fees from the Center's clients or their families.

I'm told that anyone can pay out of pocket and receive the same TLC from a local Centro de Dia.

Me, too?

"Come and talk to our doctor," suggested an energetic lady, loading the bus, when I asked her about food service. "You could come here for soup or other meals!"

Maybe those of us with legal residency can avail ourselves of services Portugal provides through these local Day Centers?

Good question!

And, given my age, I intend to ask soon.

Land of Opportunity

Mr. Green Jeans I'm not.

Far from having a green thumb, everything I try to cultivate, to grow in the ground, gives up its ghost.

Despite my best intentions, the only organisms thriving around our home are creepy crawlers and flying beasties.

Which is why we thought it practical to buy a row house without any land. It has several outdoor areas: a large covered terrace where our washing machine and laundry lines live … a cozy courtyard where we could enjoy a glass of wine, except for the dive-bombing flies and surface-surfing gnats … a balcony outside our bedroom wide enough for some potted plants and flowers, but too narrow for us to go out to tend to them … and a nook adjacent to our guest quarters, where company can sit in the shade and enjoy a good book—with that glass of wine (or a gin and tonic).

We have no land whatsoever, either enclosed yard or flowering garden. Nowhere to let the dogs out during inclement weather, when we're not inclined to take them on their long walks. No dirt to dig in, space even to support a meager herb garden … or grow Chia pet gifts for Christmas, let alone anywhere to store a metric ton of winter firewood.

Many of the folks we've met here moved to Portugal specifically to live on the land and off-the-grid. Such modern mainstays of our life – running water and indoor plumbing, air conditioning and blow dryers – are conveniences neither needed nor wanted by these robust people.

Their water comes from wells, not spigots or taps, and the wind pulls turbines rather than turbans. Fertile and flourishing, their pristine plots are filled with blossoms and blooms, yielding edibles to eat and enjoy.

And these land dwellers are probably better off because of that—certainly superior to us who, generally, dislike the color green (on cars) and have kept Tupperware in business for way too long. Where does our food come from? The refrigerator, of course!

"Quinta" ("finca" in Spanish) people are environmentally-conscious, community-minded inhabitants who have no problem slinging mud, tilling turd, picking prickly stuff off trees, or sleeping under the stars. They're the new pioneers we're more likely to find at open air markets than industrial zone Lidles, Continentes, Jumbos, or Pingo Doces.

Yes, I confess: we are homebodies, not quintaessentials.

So, imagine my shock when, walking the dogs down along our Rua do Cemitério, I came across a gated property with a "For Sale" sign posted. I spied just enough to bring up the possibility to Russ after dinner.

"Let's take a walk," I said, nonchalantly. "I want you to see something."

We walked down the street and continued around the church corner, ambling toward a part of our town we'd hardly frequented during our time here. Exactly six minutes into our hike, I stopped. We stood about four meters away from a large new house under construction.

"What do you think?" I asked, more excited now on my second visit with someone to share the thrill of something decidedly different.

"About what?" Russ replied.

"This!" I pointed, hand sweeping panoramically across the property.

"That?" he asked, looking at me quite quizzically. "It's land!"

"Yes, it is. But think of the possibilities …" Justifying and rationalizing its purchase was easy.

Fortunately, I had composed and memorized a list of attributes, which I proceeded to tick off: We'd have a place for our dogs to run around safely. Majestic fruit trees already were bursting with color, as oranges and lemons ripened throughout December (with some olives still hanging around). The rooftops of some structures (whatever they were) could be seen over the stone wall encircling the grounds, so we'd have a place to store all that firewood we'd ordered. Plus, it could increase the value of our existing property. As the real estate agents explained, "People don't want to move out here if there's no land. You don't have any." *Pièce de résistance:* We could use the property to shelter the half-dozen or so stray dogs and cats living on our village streets. And the exercise! We could become Portuguese Paul Bunyans or Johnny Appleseeds, Orangeseeds, Lemonseeds, Cherryseeds.

"What do you think?" I asked, anxious not to appear too eager.

"It's worth considering," Russ replied. "Let's see what it says on the website about it … and make arrangements to have a closer look."

We wrote down the website listed on the sign and cranked up the computer as soon as we were home. Not too big or too small – 1,000 square meters – the property had a well, several "rustic" agricultural buildings, and access to municipal water, sewer, and electricity. We completed the inquiry form online, requesting that the property be shown to us.

Arrangements were made for the property agent to meet us three days later with the keys and show us everything that came with the land.

But before, however, we came across another property online. Listed by one of the largest agencies worldwide, this one was bigger – 1,750m2 – and more expensive (€18,000). It wasn't far from where we live, but not in our village. In addition to a fully irrigated agricultural system, the land came with a small house: bedroom, bathroom, everything else room. We agreed to take a look at it the next day.

Meeting up with the property agents in the middle of Escalos de Cima, our big brother town, we followed them down a major national road and onto a paved but impossibly narrow lane for carrying two-way traffic. Fortunately, no oncoming vehicles approached during the 4.0 kms trip to the property itself. We were in the middle of nowhere, trapped, with no way out … other than to view the listing and then follow its agents. "There's another road, a wider one, that we can take back," one of them laughed as we got out of our cars and greeted the tenants on their property.

If we were looking for a quinta where we could live from the land, with well water and a composting toilet but without electricity or heat – just a generator – this may have been a place for us. But the land was to be an adjunct to our house … productive property that added land to our concrete, cement, and mortar. While the trees on this land produced 200 liters of wine, it wouldn't work for us—for too many reasons.

We learned a lot from the property agents, however, about buying and selling land: A legally-defined parcel of property in this part of Portugal (at least) is defined as an *"artigo,"* which can be further subdivided, under the proper conditions, into smaller pieces of land. Just as long as the chain of ownership and agreement could be legally documented.

Not all land is the same, we also discovered: *"rústico," "urbano,"* or agricultural could make the difference as to what could be done with it.

The more we saw of the place within walking distance in our village, the more we liked it. One-half was owned by several siblings; the other half belonged to another sibling to sell. That was *our* property! In addition to what we'd been able to see from the outside-in, we found several farm buildings – a hen house, a "smoke" room, a small pig pen or goat compartment, and a large, locked storage building with concrete floors, tiled ceilings, and cinderblock walls – all in usable condition. Friends in the village agreed that this was an ideal piece of land for us.

We made an offer. It was dismissed. We upped our offer by €1,000. It, too, was rejected. Our final offer was full price, but conditioned upon the sellers being responsible for paying all costs associated with the purchase. That offer, too, was refused.

"We are very sorry," said the property agents. "But, please, make one more offer. We will do everything possible to see that it's accepted."

What to do? So many questions! We turned to a few Facebook groups comprising expats in Portugal, seeking insights and input.

In terms of price, opinions went from one extreme to another:

Joanna started: "From the Portuguese perspective, there usually is no negotiation. The asking price is what it is and sometimes the property is on the market for a long time. The 'need' for extra money is sometimes not there and the emotional attachment plays a role."

"I know an old man selling his land for €170,000 and refused €168,000," echoed Vila. "That was five years ago and the property still is for sale."

"Rural Portuguese people have a longer perspective on the market," said Joe. "If they can't get what they want today, maybe they will get it in ten … or 70 years."

Raphaël thought differently: "Sometimes, because you are a foreigner, people expect a higher price. My advice: Don't buy. Wait. By buying too expensively, you are not only hurting yourself … local people are being hurt, too, because, when prices go up, they no longer can afford to buy property in their homeland."

Others provided additional factors: "Often, the person selling has to share between family members. If it is divided between five people, they will most likely stick to their price," explained Glenn. "Besides, sometimes they prefer to have money in a property than in the bank."

Gillian agreed: "There could be 46 family members involved and great uncle José has insisted, 'No reductions.'"

Cristina reiterated that, "many times when selling land in Portugal, it is normal for many family members to be involved in the *partilhas,* and waiting for a piece of the pie. In the case there is one who might not be willing to negotiate, the whole deal is dead."

William believed we should stick to our guns. "Land is comparatively cheap," he said.

"Wait six months," Ian urged, "they will come to you."

Victor seconded Ian's perspective: "Just don't do it. The seller smells dollars and is greedy. Most Portuguese don't have money to buy land. The seller will come back to you and I would offer less."

"Not necessarily," countered Kevin. "They will hold out for years if they don't have to sell. It's very common in Portugal."

Rather than negotiate or offer less, Julie proposed that we, "tell them we have had an offer accepted on another piece of land, but prefer theirs … and, before signing the promissory contract for the other, we're asking them to reconsider."

Mariah maintained Kevin's position: "My personal experience from 18 years in Portugal is that, often, sellers set a price that they want, which may not necessarily be reasonable or according to its market value. They will never reason or reduce their price, so, sometimes they never sell … or the property is on the market for ten years or more."

Sandra also had followed the market for years and believed that, "many would rather not sell than to lower a price they already think is low. Some don't have any urgency on selling, so they can have the property out on the market until someone pays the required price. It's not only what the buyer is willing to pay that runs Portugal's property market, but also what the seller is willing to take."

Someone asked an interesting question that we hadn't considered: How did we know for certain that the property agents actually had presented our offer to the sellers? Maybe they hadn't and were holding out for a better offer from us, which would boost their commission? Other than their word, what proof did we have that our offers weren't rejected … just never presented by the agents to the sellers?

Good question!

And what about the "status" and potential of the property?

There's a difference between land identified as "rústico" and that which is "urbano." You can build on the latter, but not necessarily on the former.

Although the property agent had listed the land for sale as *"terreno rústico,"* her marketing materials stated, *"Terreno onde poderá construer a sua morada de sonho"* (land where you can build the house of your dreams).

Could we build on it, if we decided to downsize? If so, on how much of it and where? Again, we turned to our Facebook groups for advice.

"We have an *artigo rústico* which has a section where construction is permitted and, according to the local development plan (PDN), we could apply for planning permission," posted Phillippa, explaining that the rest of her land is protected. "If you go to the *Cámara* (council) where the land is located, you can find out exactly what is allowed."

João was a more specific about the language used in the listing and way the land was described: "It doesn't really say, 'you can build,' but, 'you may be able to build' … and that's lost in the translation. *"Onde pode"* (present tense) means "where you can," while *"onde poderá"* (future tense) implies that you may be able to. Like others, he suggested that we check with the *Cámara* about whether we could get the necessary permits to build a house to live in on the land.

Even more precise was Daniela:

"Whether a piece of land is urbano or rústico has nothing to do with being able to build on it or not—it merely has to do with the way that specific piece of land is registered in the *'registo predial.'* The only way you can find out if you can build on it or not – and how much you can potentially build – is asking the estate agents for the plot code from the *registo predial* … and then taking that to the *Cámara* and asking them to check what type of land it is and if it allows you to build on it or not."

"Also," she added, "a piece of land might be *rústico* and have a ruin on it, which may be marked on the blueprint of the property in the *registo*. If it is, you are allowed to renovate it … but, obviously, you would need to obtain the required licenses, approvals, etc."

Ultimately, it was Jill's advice that meshed most neatly with our own plans: "I would make an offer … but, subject to the condition that – before purchase – the agent and/or the owner has the title of part of the land changed from *rústico* to *urbano."*

That's what we did, offering €1,000 less than the asking price.

This time, our offer was accepted, with conditions:

The seller wanted us to agree to a lower purchase price (on paper) for tax reasons. We'd also need to wait four months to go to settlement – and get the deed – until all of the "disengagement" was completed.

We agreed, although we had a few stipulations of our own: We would do nothing illegal, in terms of selling the property for less (on paper) than we actually paid; we asked for an itemized account of what our "closing" costs would be, especially if we were agreeing – on paper – to a lower purchase price; we wanted a bona fide, good faith estimate of what our closing costs on the property would be; we asked that the portion this land with existing structures, listed as *"rústico,"* but where "the house of our dreams could be built," be legally changed to *"urbano";* and we insisted that an authorized property map be prepared and signed by the *Cámara,* showing its exact measurements, boundaries, and percentage (or specific square meters) where new property could be built, based upon the local public "PDN."

We believe we will have made a wise investment.

In addition to enjoying the benefits of the nearby land and its structures, by adding 1,000m2 of land a short walk from our house, we have increased its value substantially.

Whether we're able to grow anything remains to be

seen. But at least we'll have chickens in the coop … hopefully laying eggs.

Portugal indeed is a land of opportunity.

And we're now its newest landed gentry.

Creature Comforts

With all due respect to our UK friends and American acquaintances who live in Portugal's bigger cities and Spain's metropolises – or, at least, in more upscale dwellings than ours – we who make our homes in the small towns and villages of these two Iberia countries lack and may covet what you probably have that we don't: creature comforts.

I'm talking about petite pleasures and little luxuries like central heating, mold-free residences, bug barriers, food without flies, and gnats not whining in your ears. Wouldn't it be nice not to wipe down our digs daily because a layer of grit always appears overnight, sprinkling silt and dust bunnies on table tops, furniture and floors!

Most of all, however, I'm referring to the pure delight of starting my days with long, luxurious, hot, über strong showers.

By now, you know that we're people who enjoy our home and its assorted creature comforts.

Along with our "creatures" – three Miniature Schnauzers – we work, eat, sleep, shower, and attend to life's necessities in two adjoining rooms measuring no more than 40-square-meters (combined). In other words, about two-thirds of our time is spent in a concrete and plaster crucible with windows but zero, zilch, insulation. Nada.

Which is why we mop and dust daily.

We indulged ourselves and invested in an 18,000 BTU inverter air conditioning unit that, according to our research, is the most cost-effective and efficient way to keep us warm during the cold times, yet cooler if it's hot. We set it at 19° C (66° F) when the temperature falls … and 24° C (75° F) once the heat hits those shades of hades.

Yes, I know that we pay a steep price for such succor, with monthly electric (EDP) bills averaging 150 Euros for a three-story, 125m2 house.

Which brings me to my current rant:

We need to replace our (gas-fired) water heater.

It's bad enough that the infernal contraption is located up in our attic and almost impossible to reach ... that each canister of propane fueling it weighs over 75 pounds and costs €26.40 in Portugal, a lot less in Spain ... and getting the canister up those misplaced steps into the attic, where it requires the contortions of two Cirque du Soleil performers to lift it up the stairs ... roll it across the attic's cement floor ... stand it up again ... and connect it to the water heater on the far side.

All of which wouldn't be quite so awful, except that:

• We never know when the hot water is going to give up and run out, but it usually happens while I'm in the middle of a shower and need to shout my partner out of a deep sleep and a warm bed to venture up to the attic and change the canister;

• To achieve maximum heat from the water it outputs, the pressure setting must be dialed down; and

• When all is said and done, the shower water is still but a drizzle of tepid, lukewarm water at best—and certainly not forceful enough to rinse the shampoo out of hair, shaving lather from a face, or soap off one's skin.

We'd been going through three gas cylinders that serve only our bathroom's sink and shower every month. Adding insult to injury, there's always – always! – unproductive propane still in the tank.

The lady who owns the corner mini-market where we exchange our depleted "botijas" for refills shakes her head "não," wagging her finger. She explains emphatically (in Portuguese too rapid for me) that gas should only be used in the kitchen for cooking. Water, she insists, should be heated electrically.

"But the electric is so expensive here ..." I counter.

She shrugs. And asks, "E aquelas?" referring to the three propane tanks we go through each month. "Quanto custam?"

How much are we spending every month on those propane canisters?

Eighty euros, more or less!

Would our electric bills increase more than that if we were to replace the gas water heater with an electric one?

She doesn't know, but suggests I ask EDP (the electric company), an electrician, or the appliance store where we buy the new unit.

Fortunately, we've got a great electrodomésticos (appliance) shop managed by a good-looking guy who knows his stuff – he's actually "energy-certified!" – and explains the problem to us: Because the weather is colder, it requires more gas to heat the water. And since it's coldest in the attic where the water heater is located, we're not getting our money's worth out of the propane. Always, some will remain.

Handsome João concurs that an electric water heater will serve our purposes better … and operating it should cost less than the €80 we've been spending on gas monthly, even with the 120 liter capacity model recommended for three people taking back-to-back showers.

We buy the unit and make arrangements for it to be installed, which include having electricity brought up to the attic. All should be ready to use in another week or so (probably "or so," this being Portugal).

Until then, we will dash down a flight of steps every morning in our terrycloth robes to avail ourselves of the guest bedroom shower.

We'll also do battle with water on another front: the mold.

The most common causes of mold growing on walls and ceilings here are high humidity, condensation, and water leaks (often hidden inside the walls or ceilings). Check. Check. Check. In houses like ours, it's not uncommon to have all three. Condensation forms when water vapor in the air meets cold surfaces and cools to become liquid. Leaking pipes near or inside of walls are a common cause of mold.

Say "hello" to typical home construction in Portugal and Spain!

A bottle with bleach in hand, we spray the ceilings and walls whenever we notice any "damp" (as our British friends call it) shadow appearing. During colder times, especially, we move furniture away from the walls and take our clothing off the wardrobe rods that come in contact with walls. After a heavy dose of bleach solution, we follow up with special "anti-moho" spray and let the areas dry for 24 hours.

After the rainy season, we'll need to have a new €7,000 roof installed: a special "sandwich" with insulation between the metal top and bottom, it should cut down on the leaks and the moisture—along with the mold. It would also keep us warmer, reducing the electricity consumed by our aircon and new water heater.

Despite spending a bundle on our new roof and water heater, we're counting on all the money we'll be saving on our EDP bills.

Uh-huh.

The flies and the gnats are gathering already in anticipation.

City Dogs, Country Cães
(A Children's Story)

Three beloved Miniature Schnauzers – Jax: a white male, Sheba: a black female, and Manny: a silver-gray male – moved with their family from a cold climate in the upper Midwest of the United States to a new home in a small village of central Portugal.

When they finally arrived at their destination after three long airplane flights and almost a full day traveling, all three dogs were insecure. "Where are we?" they wondered. "What happened to the rooms and smells – the world – we loved and lived in for so long?"

Now, they had pet passports that allowed them to travel from country to country throughout the European Union, and licenses which recognized them in their own Portuguese village.

Their human daddies did everything they could to comfort and reassure them. In addition to packing their favorite keepsakes to bring along, the dogs had new beds and bedding, plenty of good food to eat, squeaky toys to play with, and the attention of their two devoted dads.

One day not long after the dogs arrived, their dads fastened leashes onto the dogs' collars and took them for a long walk around the village. Suddenly, they came across three other dogs in the street.

"Bow-Wow-Wow!" greeted Gonçalo the Galgo.

"Woof, Woof, Woof!" welcomed Pedro the Podengo.

"Bark, Bark, Bark!" began María, mistress of the streets.

But Manny, Sheba, and Jax could not understand a word they were saying, because the other dogs were speaking Portuguese … and the three American dogs had not yet learned that language.

So, they just wagged their tails with excitement.

Later that same day, the American dogs were out on their afternoon walk when the three Portuguese dogs came running over to them.

All of the dogs were happy to meet again and discovered that, by listening carefully, they were able to understand the words and the motions shared by each other. It was a common language!

The Portuguese dogs introduced themselves first.

"Boa tarde," said Gonçalo. "I am a galgo, a dog used for racing and hunting—for only one season … but then I was discarded." Tears filled Gonçalo's eyes, as he continued his sad story: "I was starved before hunting, to make me more hungry for the prey."

Jax, Manny, and Sheba couldn't imagine a life like that.

Pedro spoke next: "Podengos are even more persecuted than galgos. Curious and clownish, we are very aware of our surroundings and very sensitive to humans. We are wonderful family members! But, like Gonçalo, I came from a breeder who chained me and sold me for sport. I was abused, treated badly, and abandoned because I wouldn't kill."

The three American dogs felt very sad for their new friends. Though shaggy and unkempt – their teeth needed cleaning and they all could benefit by baths – the Portuguese dogs were welcoming and outgoing.

"When I was young and just a pretty little puppy, I was a Christmas gift to two little children," María explained." She had fond memories of their times together, until she grew bigger and they were older. A few years later, the family moved, leaving María behind—without even a hug good-bye or words of farewell. Closing the door to the house where they lived one last time, they left María on the street. Over the years, she had given birth to many litters of puppies … but no longer could remember what had happened to them or where they went.

Licking their new friends with their tongues to make them feel better, the American dogs said, "Até breve," because their daddies were ready to return home and the dogs wanted to see the dogs again soon.

Eating dinner in the warmth of their kitchen, the three American dogs talked about their new friends.

"Where do they live?" asked Jax.

"Who takes care of them and feeds them?" wondered Sheba.

"What do they do during the days and nights, while we're taking our naps?" Manny inquired.

Eager to learn more about their lives, the American dogs decided to bring bits of their food as treats for their Portuguese amigos.

Early the next morning, right after their breakfast, leashes and collars were put on Jax, Sheba, and Manny. Their dads opened the front door, as the dogs scampered along, tugging at their leashes.

Where were María, Pedro, and Gonçalo?

Turning the corner and walking past the garbage bins (where Manny and Jax lifted their legs), they could hear the voices of their friends coming from farther down the street. But there were other voices, too.

"Olá, amigos," said Pedro upon seeing his English-speaking friends from America. "I want you to meet Francisco, Ana, Rodrigo, Miguel, Patricia, and Tomás. They live in this village, too!"

"You do? Where?" Sheba and Manny responded immediately. "Why haven't we seen you before? It's great to have so many friends!"

Gonçalo explained that the other dogs lived with families in houses and only were put outside a few times each day.

"But, but ..." The American dogs didn't know what to ask first.

"Your families don't walk you with leashes?" Manny wanted to know. "Aren't you afraid to walk by yourselves with all these cars and trucks on the streets? How do you pick up after yourselves?"

"We don't!" exclaimed Rodrigo. "Sometimes the rain washes it away. Other times, it just stays here, until it dries up. Often, cars drive over it, pushing it down between the cobble stones. You dogs from America have servants who clean and pick up after you, no?"

Sheba was anxious and wanted her question to be answered: "All those vehicles are going in both directions so fast! Aren't you afraid?"

"Oh, you get used to it," Ana and Patricia nodded. "Usually, they'll slow down if they see you … but sometimes you need to run to a spot in a doorway, against the wall, or between cars, and wait for them to pass."

Patricia and Ana lived together with the same family. They heard the mother calling their names, so they scampered off. "Adeus," they said, wishing the newcomers well. Rodrigo, Miguel, Tomás, amd Francisco followed the girls, leaving the Americans with their three first friends.

"Where do you live?" Jax asked María, Pedro, and Gonçalo.

"Right here," Pedro responded. "We live on the streets."

"But who takes care of you? Who feeds you? Where do you sleep? What do you drink?" concerned Jax, the eldest dog of his family.

"We can take care of ourselves," grinned Gonçalo with pride. "The water from the village fountain is always plentiful and quite good."

"People throw table scraps onto the street for us … pieces of fish, chicken, and even meat," piped in Pedro. "Cats rip open the plastic trash bags, but we chase them away and find food there, too. Some people are really nice: They buy food for us at the grocery store and put it outside, on the street, for us to eat. That's really convenient, eating food on the street—right next to where we sleep."

"Food from the street? Food on the street? That's where you eat?" asked Manny, trying to imagine eating like that.

The American dogs were on low-fat diets. Yet, compared to their new Portuguese friends, they were very well fed. Their dads mixed together special dry food from bags with moist dog food from cans. Then, tiny pieces of boiled chicken breasts with rice – along with fresh pumpkin or squash – were cooked, pureed, and placed in plastic containers in the freezer or refrigerator … until they were needed. Everything would be mixed together: some of this with some of that. Why, it took almost twenty minutes just for the food to be mixed in their stainless steel bowls, which were picked up and washed as soon as the dogs finished eating their meals.

"You sleep on the street?" Sheba cried, her motherly instincts kicking in. "Aren't you cold? Or hot in the summers? What about all the bugs, flies, and mosquitoes? Don't they bite? Won't you get sick?"

"Não," answered Pedro, muzzling María. "We watch out for each other. Often, we curl up together to sleep. That's nice and warm. When it's not raining, we find a welcome mat to lie on …. if it rains, we will sleep under the parked cars."

Usually shy, María began to speak:

"You Americans have many questions. We tried, our best, to answer them. Now it's our turn. Can we ask you some questions?"

"Of course," echoed Manny, Sheba, and Jax … all at once.

"What are those colorful tags, decorating your necklaces?" she asked. "Do you always wear jewelry like that?"

"Oh, they're not necklaces," laughed Sheba, "but collars attached to our leashes. And the tags on them show that we have been vaccinated by the veterinarian against diseases that flies and worms and mosquitoes can spread. Haven't you had shots to keep you safe, too?"

The Portuguese dogs shook their heads, explaining that they were from the same land and were not bothered by their bites. As foreigners and newcomers to their environment, however, the American dogs would need to be protected from such pests and diseases.

"And we all must be careful to avoid the processionary caterpillars," warned Gonçalo. "They are dangerous to us all!"

185

"Hey, don't those collars and leashes bother you?" María doubted. "How can you run and roam if you're always attached to them?"

Jax scratched his head before responding, "We can't. Why would we want to race around town, anyway? We're perfectly happy walking with our dads. They're looking for a piece of land now near our house, so that we can run around safely. Before moving here, we always had a yard where we could go outside to play and do ... stuff," he said.

"You mean that you never travel or go anywhere without people?" Pedro wondered. "Like there ..." He lifted his leg and pointed his paw toward the snow-capped tops of the distant Serra mountains.

"We've traveled a lot with our family," sniffed Sheba. "But we always go by plane or car, in the back with seat belts. We've been on vacation to Porto, we go to the groomer in the big city, and we have a holiday home in Spain, where we know lots of dogs who speak Spanish ... a language not unlike Portuguese. Their lives are similar to yours, although more of them walk with leashes held by people now. And snow? We've seen lots of it. In fact, we played in the snow quite often. One of the places we lived before moving here was Wisconsin, where there's so much snow that, sometimes, it's higher than us!"

"But you can only go where your family takes you," remarked the Portuguese dogs. "Even in our village, there are so many delightful places to visit, sights to see, and smells to enjoy!"

Like a shadow, a thoughtful silence fell over the dogs for a moment.

"Yes," Jax admitted. "That is true. But we'd rather be with our family than out and about without them. They take such good care of us. So, seeing and smelling what's here isn't that important. We're happy!"

"Well ... since you mention it," reacted María, "it appears your family does take very good care of you. Maybe too good? Are they feeding you too much? Is that

186

good for your health? And, look at your nails!"

"Our nails?" all three American dogs gasped.

While the Portuguese dogs sorely needed baths and haircuts, their nails were neat and trim. How was that?

"Because of the cobble stone streets in the village," Pedro explained.

The American dogs had walked only on soft grass, so their nails had to be trimmed by a groomer. They didn't like that at all! And their wet feet always were wiped off with the towel by the front door.

"What I want to know," Gonçalo interrupted, "is who will take care of you if your family is gone? When or if your dads aren't here?"

Suddenly, all of the dogs – Portuguese and American – were sad, as they thought about their lives and the people they loved.

At the end of the week, after several very long conversations where they all learned new languages, the friendly dogs went back again to where they lived. Although the American dogs regretted that they didn't have the freedom to come and go as the Portuguese dogs did, they truly loved their families and appreciated their comfortable lives.

Waving good-bye to their Portuguese friends until later, the American dogs realized that their lives might be different from how their friends lived, but that they really were not any better than them.

"We are quite fortunate," they said to each other, as their new friends bounded off down the street after a cat that had come out from under one of the cars.

"Até logo!"

Bonfires of Humanity

A burning bush.

According to the biblical narrative, that's where Moses met God. After calling out from the bush, the Scriptures say of the Exodus that, "By day the LORD went ahead of them in a pillar of cloud to guide them on their way and by night in a pillar of fire to give them light."

Deities are associated with fire and worship in African, Asian, European, Middle Eastern, and Native American mythology.

Chariots of fire, not Christmas trees or crèches, are found throughout the Judeo-Christian heritage. Fire figures conspicuously in Christianity, most prominently at Pentecost: "And there appeared to them tongues as of fire, distributed and resting on each one of them."

Celebrating Christmas with yuletide bonfires has a history of spiritual precedents ... not that such exegesis is particularly important to the Spanish or Portuguese people.

Let's face it, folks: the Christmas holidays are traditionally a mixture of Christian rites and pagan rituals.

In the heart of Portugal, the inland region, Christmas Eve is marked by a ceremony known as the "burning of the yuletide log" where the town stands together and sings around a fire, fostering community spirit, enjoying some wine ... and helping to keep the baby Jesus warm.

From the rivalry between villages (having the greatest, most beautiful bonfire is worth celebrating), firewood was sometimes stolen by young boys. Today, their parents pay for it.

Penamacor's Christmas *Madeiros,* a festivity that begins with a procession of tractors carrying several tons of wood to build a huge pile – often reaching more than 10 meters high – consists of lighting a huge bonfire around which people will gather for days (and nights).

Spain has its own sizzling Christmas customs.

A truly unique one, *Hogueras de Navidad,* is a pagan ritual celebrated primarily in Granada and Jaen on

December 21st. According to folklore, people who jump over fires on the shortest day of the year (winter solstice) will be protected from illness. So, that's exactly what they do.

Along with figurines "defecating" in nativity scenes, the Catalans have *Tió de Nadal,* a jolly Christmas log which they stick in the fireplace every Christmas Eve. Tradition says you must order *Tío Nadal* to "poop" while spanking him with a stick. The ever-smiling tree trunk then waits for the youngsters to go to bed before bringing them their gifts.

After the midnight mass *(La Misa de Gallo),* people stroll through Spanish streets carrying torches, playing guitars, beating tambourines and drums. *"Esta noche es la noche buena ... y no es noche de dormir,"* goes the saying: Tonight is the good night; it is not meant for sleeping!

Nowadays in Spain, there's a much different reason for not sleeping.

Occurring on December 22 and held every year since 1812, the Spanish National Lottery is a really big deal at Christmas. Almost everyone plays, making it the world's biggest lottery. In terms of the huge amounts of cash that can be won, so big is Spain's Christmas Lottery that it's been nicknamed *"El Gordo"* ("the fat one"), whose winning numbers are sung out by school children.

In terms of the true meaning of Christmas, big, fat, blazing bonfires and burning logs are more meaningful to me than church services focusing on a rehearsed repertoire of candy cane carols and Nativity legends.

The truth behind those beloved stories?

• **Christmas is about believing what a woman said about her sex life.** Mary spoke openly and honestly about it. So did Dr. Christine Blasey Ford, who accused (now) U.S. Supreme Court Justice Brett Kavanaugh of sexual misconduct. While many others hearken the #MeToo cry, our norms need to treat women more respectfully and responsibly.

• **Christmas is about a family finding safety as asylum**

seekers. En route to a census at Joseph's hometown, Mary gave birth in Bethlehem. Though there was no room at the inn for the migrants, they were given shelter in a barn where, surrounded by farm animals, they felt secure. How many thousands of asylum-seeking families have been separated from their children, political pawns in a gruesome game of thrones?

• **Christmas is about a child in need receiving support from the wealthy.** Not only was hospitality allotted to Jesus and his family, but legendary shepherds, wise men, and even kings paid him homage with their salutations, honor, and gifts. Can the richest countries this world has ever known do any less for our children—borne and thereafter? From education to health, food and child welfare, we must care.

• **Christmas is about God identifying with the marginalized.** Who did Jesus acknowledge and associate throughout his life? Not the privileged or the powerful!

"For I was hungry and you gave me something to eat, I was thirsty and you gave me something to drink, I was a stranger and you invited me in, I needed clothes and you clothed me, I was sick and you looked after me, I was in prison and you came to visit me. Truly I tell you, whatever you did for one of the least of these brothers and sisters of mine, you did for me."

Why do we honor, commemorate, someone's birth?

"In the end, you will not see the physical beauty in others that caught your eye, but the fire that burned within them. This kind of beauty is the bonfire you had to attend."

So says inspirational author Shannon L. Alder.

Like bonfires and burning logs, Christmas and birthday memorials help us to keep those beloved in our hearts alive and ablaze in our minds.

The real "miracle" of the Christmas story is that the divine is expressed all around us in the everyday, commonplace elements of our lives.

Foreigners or Extraterrestrials?

Expats, immigrants, refugees, aliens.

What's the difference between these labels and social identifiers?

It basically depends on your viewpoint.

"I emigrated from Portugal to the United States when I was a kid," Luís shares. "No question, I wasn't an expat … but an immigrant, pure and simple. Now I returned here to Portugal, having felt totally American for the last 50 years. I don't think I'm an immigrant back here, but an expat fish living out of water. I'm neither expat nor immigrant now!"

Given our circumstances and condition, is one word more correct or appropriate than another? Where's the double-edge sword, that fine line dividing the spirit and soul of these expressions, I wondered.

In discussion with Luís and others about these terms, I realized that many people interpret or use them differently. To me it was simple: One self-identifies as an expat … but is deemed an immigrant, refugee, and/or alien by others: government, institutions, bureaucrats, people. We debated the implications of these words, as well as their usage.

Does it have to do with one's political, legal, economic, geographic, racial, or social status? Or a philosophical orientation, a state of mind?

Is it, perhaps, a matter of choice? A designation conferred or assumed? A product of our past, present, or future plans and projections?

Maybe it's actually about where one is coming from … and arriving at?

"I consider myself an expat from the UK and an immigrant in/to Portugal," bilaterally admits Keith.

Perhaps it has more to do with times and the timing? Is your stay away temporary or permanent? How long you're away from your homeland will determine whether you're deemed an "immigrant" or "expat."

If you come here on vacation and invest in a holiday home, but your residence is elsewhere … or you take an assignment for work, short- or long-term, you are an expat, goes this argument. Those who live here and no longer have residences in another country are immigrants.

"Expat, in my eyes, is someone who goes to live in a foreign country to work, but will return after her contract is finished," expounds Pamela. "I will never go back to live in my home country, so I am an immigrant."

It all boils down to intention: You have no have intention to live here permanently? You stay six months to a couple of years? Call yourself an expat. You're here and never intend to go back? You're an immigrant.

This difference is a very personal one for Karen: "I grew up as an expat kid, someone who lived overseas as a result of my father's work. That isn't an immigrant—we never planned to stay. Prior to coming to Portugal, I lived in another country, this time because of my husband's work. Still, I had no plans of staying there. Now that I'm in Portugal – hopefully, forever! – I see myself as an immigrant."

Is one a term of endearment, another an attitude and prejudice?

Are the words pejorative, judgment suggested in their usage?

"Yes," agreed one in the group, "there's a distribution from positive to negative: expat > immigrant > refugee."

Expat "often assumes money and choice," whereas immigrant "can be taken more adversely," presupposing a financial hardship or other desperate need to move to a new country.

Some say that racism also plays a role: Are people of color called one thing, while whites are deemed another? After all, how many African expats do you know?

Many feel the term "expat" is just another way in which white privilege is manifested, since, often, the image of an immigrant is a person of color, while the expat is a hip, white American or European.

Essentially, most insist, it's always an aspect of intention.

Expats are intentional people who choose to move for reasons other than safety and asylum. They're people who move to other countries to work, travel, study, enjoy the weather ... while those who emigrate from their own country to live evermore in another are immigrants.

If you don't intend to return to your homeland, you're an immigrant. You're an expat if you are going back (or intend to) to your birth place.

Some non-nationals react unenthusiastically to the word "expat," as they say it connotes a certain cachet and sense of superiority.

"Expat has a negative connotation to me, as in many places, they are people (often in corporate or government jobs) who fail to integrate, preferring to mix with people from their country of origin," maintained one ardent immigrant. "They live far better than the natives, employing local drivers, maids, and guards ... but, otherwise, do not socialize much with the local community."

For me and most of the English-speaking people I know here in Portugal (and Spain), however, that's simply not the case.

We don't want to live in self-exiled enclaves, ghettos of our own device. We've chosen to live where we do so that our friends are local natives, the language spoken is theirs, the houses our families now inhabit lack the conveniences and comforts we've taken for granted, we walk more than drive, our diet no longer is so rich and fat.

And we have no intention of returning to live in America. Maybe to visit or because of a family emergency, but not to reside there again.

Culturally derived or arrogantly applied, the irony is that I see myself as an expat, not an immigrant. I will always be connected to America, concerned about its policies and welfare, participating actively in the country's political process, and voting—albeit from here.

Is the title of my book – *EXPAT: Leaving the USA for Good* – inherently wrong? Based on the opinions of others, our intention to reside here and not return to the USA makes us immigrants, not expats.

Expat vs. immigrant.

Someone summed it up quite nicely: "It's just semantics. Essentially, expat and immigrant are the same. While both are living in a country they weren't born in, one has made a lifetime move while the other is living outside his or her home country … but not forever."

Others believe that "expat" is a term used almost exclusively by Americans living abroad because a country conceived by immigrants cannot comprehend someone leaving the USA for another country.

"In the end, it's an ideologically grounded word that was mostly used in the Cold War for Americans who went to places like Czechoslovakia and France," remarked that same someone during the conversation.

When I was younger and we lived in a black-and-white world, I worried about what I should be, rather than who I was. Popeye the sailor man, a cartoon character, had a motto, which proved to be true: "I am what I am, and that's all that I am."

There is a lot of meaning in that scrappy sentence.

Even if we don't eat spinach!

Facebook Fracas

First, let me confess: It's my fault and I take the blame.

Growing increasingly frustrated, annoyed, amazed, and furious at all the high crimes and felonies (never mind misdemeanors) Donald Trump & Company have been getting away with so far in their power plays, executive privileges, and assumed presidential powers, I quite clearly posted derision on my Facebook feed:

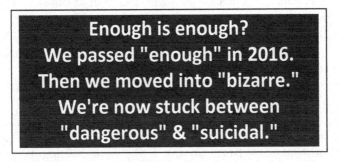

Enough is enough?
We passed "enough" in 2016.
Then we moved into "bizarre."
We're now stuck between
"dangerous" & "suicidal."

Immediately, the reactions and responses began flowing from around the world. Some thought that, as someone who chose to move away from the USA, what happened in my homeland should no longer matter to me. I – and others – strongly disagreed … as you'll see from the posts copied from Facebook below. To protect privacy and personal space, I will, wherever possible, use first names only.

Susan: I barely know how to contribute to the solution anymore. Guess it's communicating with representatives to push the wiser agendas.

Bruce: But are they listening and responding, Susan? Communication is a two-way street!

Jan: They DO respond, but it takes a lot of pushing from a load of folks. We've reversed some big policies here in Houston and nationally. And replaced some Republicans where we could. Meanwhile, 2020 Trump campaign is already in full swing, expecting to spend up to $1 billion! And a database of 60 million people's cells developed through ad campaigns, etc. Can we compete? We have to!

Tsvika: With all due respect, Bruce, wasn't part of the point of moving away to stop caring about these things?

Bruce: With all due respect, Tsvika, "you can take the boy out of the country, but never the country out of the boy." While our lives are much better and happier here, we will never stop caring about the welfare of our brothers and sisters, our families and friends, in the USA ... we won't turn our backs on them and will continue to be proactive — from Portugal and Spain — in bringing about change for the better.

Tsvika: By posting on Facebook and perhaps submitting mail-in ballots that won't get counted?

Bruce: Yes. That and anything else we can do to make a difference.

Susan: Our responsibility as U.S. citizens doesn't end when we move overseas. It's possible we do MORE than most persons based in the U.S., from helping people register to vote to doing call-banks to writing or calling our legislators. What's happening in the U.S. affects us greatly, from taxes to investment rates to the impact being made across the world, not to mention the fall of value in the U.S. dollar against the Euro.

Tsvika: If you feel so responsible, Susan, why did you move away?

Bruce: One can move away for a better life ... or for whatever reason. But that doesn't mean you forget where you came from or the debt that you owe to your forbearers and those we left behind.

Tsvika: Then, by that same logic, a parent who abandons a child feels more responsibility for it? I'm sorry, it doesn't make sense. I get your sentimental stance, but don't run away from the problem and then complain about how bad it is. It can't help but raise the (very understandable) critique of hypocrisy.

Bruce: To refer to my position as a "sentimental stance," and then accuse me of hypocrisy ("don't run away from the problem and then complain about how bad it is") is anathema and repugnant to me. We live in a connected world, where we all must be conduits.

Joshua: How does one forget where they lived? How does one simply leave behind when there's so much to save? How does one ignore such a huge problem? No matter where you are or what your intentions, you'll always have feelings for the place where you begin.

Tsvika: I guess as someone who only very rarely feels that way, Joshua, it's hard for me to relate.

Milu: How can someone forget their roots? How can you expect Bruce to ignore what is happening in his homeland? It doesn't matter what he chose to do with where he wants to live. He is still a USA citizen who loves his country and therefore hurts with the present situation. It's only normal! How can you love your country and approve of the terrible path it is taking? It's because you love it that you raise your voice and condemn this behavior. Like a good parent would do to a child that is choosing wrong paths!

Bruce: Thank you, Milu. Tsvika lives in Lisbon, Portugal, now. But he's also lived in Pittsburgh, Chicago, Berlin, and Tel Aviv. Perhaps he's a man without a country ... or that proverbial "Flying Dutchman?"

Amy: American expats, if voting correctly as UOCAVA voters vs. general mail-in (citizens in-country who are unable to go to the polls on voting day or, as in many and a growing number of states, who all vote by mail), our votes are legally required to be counted (along with military) ... and have been.

Linda: For those who understand abstract constructs like patriotism, loyalty, family and betrayal, this probably isn't necessary. For others that don't have a firm grasp of these concepts, let me use a metaphor:

Imagine you come from a family that is warm, nurturing and has a strong foundation to help not just you, but many members of your family to succeed and thrive. It is a family filled with warmth, love, song, structure and maybe even prayer and faith. Sure, sometimes Mom and Dad fight. Your sister goes through a rebellious phase. Your cousin gets in that bad car wreck and is in a coma for three days. But, for the most part, it's a strong family with a decent foundation and you love your family completely and totally ... there's nothing you wouldn't do for them.

As time goes on – maybe it's because your thoughts mature – or maybe because things really do change ... but as time goes on, you become aware of cracks in the foundation. Maybe you start to notice that Dad drinks a little too much or shouts a little too loudly at the TV. Mom becomes less focused on the family and her attention turns elsewhere. Your sister develops a drug habit and your brother spends most of his time on the Internet, engaging in conspiracy theories.

But these are the people who raised you. Your love and loyalty to them is not in doubt. Ever.

Then, one day, there's a betrayal. Your sister steals some money from you – money that you would have gladly given or loaned. Mom throws a pan at Dad and hits him in the head during an argument. Dad spends more time at the bar. The next thing you know, Mom and Dad are divorcing, your sister is a full-on opioid addict, and your brother has joined a cult.

Holy crap! What the hell happened to your strong, loving family? Your sister steals more from you, Mom and Dad's relationship becomes toxic and they try to draw you into it. Your brother uses his car to run over somebody he disagreed with and has started spouting some real Nazi rhetoric. He starts bringing his Nazi friends home and they begin to look sideways at your gay, black friend ... who no longer feels comfortable in your house and stops coming around.

Now, maybe those cracks were always there and you didn't notice. Or maybe they've just recently developed. But the fact of the matter is, they are there now and you've got to deal with it. How they got there doesn't matter.

You work hard to bring the family back together. Sure,

maybe you complain about it online and you appeal to a higher authority to help change your family back. But your keyboard typing does nothing (except help you understand your emotions and feelings) and you connect with other people whose families are equally messed up, so you share thoughts, ideas, and whatever else. The higher authority you appeal to says that all of your complaints are coming to his office because somebody "on the other side" has paid you to call his office. You're not really his constituent.

So your family is falling apart, has become physically dangerous for your friend due to your brother's Nazi friends, and you begin to feel for your own sanity if you continue to live in that house where the pots and pans are flying. You are also concerned either about being caught in the crossfire between your family members or becoming a direct target if you continue to try to guide them back to the family you used to be.

So you move. Across town, across the state, across the world. And when you're in your new house, you call your mom and ask how things are going. Still pretty crappy.

But do you stop caring? NO! OMG, NO! How can you even imagine that moving away to preserve your own sanity means you no longer care?

You still encourage your sister to go to rehab. You beg Mom and Dad to seek marital counseling. Or, at least, ask them to try to part amicably. Your brother ... who knows how to even reach him, but you'll never stop trying, right? And you continue to call your representative to try to get help. And when that person can't or won't help you, you wait for him (or her) to come up for election. You vote them out and vote somebody else in, who, at least, says she'll help your family. And help in the ways that you think will work, not somebody who says they'll just pour gas on your house and burn it down.

Patriotism. Loyalty. Pride in one's country. These aren't things that disappear just because you've chosen to put a little healthy distance between you and the problems.

People are flawed. Countries are even more flawed. But

it's a rare person who can simply walk away from that which is a foundational part of their very being or psyche. You'll never stop caring. You'll never stop loving. And you'll NEVER stop trying to get your family to be that which you know it can.

Bruce: Linda, OMG! You have made me cry, expressing – poignantly yet precisely – how so many of us feel ...

Susan: I disliked this post since Tsvika took it off course ... or, maybe he put it on course and as a result we have Linda's comment. That, if only that, was worth turning that corner.

Mark: To extend Linda's analogy, I am a Brit, with 25 years, two marriages, a daughter, many friends, and a number of properties in the USA. I am not a U.S. citizen, but I am a green card holder. Perhaps I have "married-in" to this dysfunctional family that Linda portrayed. Therefore, I have a vested interest in the U.S., and in its problems. This interest will not change when I relocate to Portugal.

While I do not vote in the United Sates, I have been politically, socially, and economically active there. I provide housing to low-income renters, some of whom are on government support, many from minority groups. I have tried to steer American views as away from the dismal abyss that it has now plunged into ... but to no avail.

I fear for my disabled daughter and gay/atheist/minority friends who will remain in Gilead after I am gone. I already have offered many of them a path to Portugal in the hope that they, too, can escape the fundamentally dangerous idiocrasy of the current regime.

None of these people want to "give up" on the U.S. They all care about what the country has become and how it is treating people inside and outside its borders. They will continue to vote, and be politically active; for their own safety and sanity, however, they have decided to do it from outside the reach of the despot-in-chief.

Jan: Check to make sure your ballots get counted with local Dem office. They can pull up your voting record. Where you live doesn't prevent you from caring or defending democracy! This is a world phenomenon coming to a theater near you, too! I know this is mainly a discussion about the feelings of loss, love, and imperiled connections. But a safe distance doesn't impair your ability to be proactive and helpful. Definitely, we can make a difference—from wherever we are!

Linda B: It's the "Twilight Zone". If everyone cared, universally, then maybe the petty differences won't show up so quickly. Because we pay taxes, have property, vote, in the USA doesn't mean we should shackle our lives there. Adventure is good; learning new languages and ways is good; having a broader scope of the world is good.

Susan: I enjoy the sentiment of your comment, Linda.

Margaret: I bet you try not to pay attention, but it is like watching a car crash while happening. You are not in the car, but you want to know where the pieces are going to end up ... so they don't land on you.

Regina: The world's population needs to care and pay attention!

Amy: There are many reasons people choose to live in a different country than their homeland. Don't assume, Tsvika, that every person has the single same reason - to escape and forget about it. That is short-sighted and close-minded.

Vickie: Sorry, guys, if you can no longer vote, you really can't bring about change.

Bruce: But we can – and do – vote, Vickie. All the time! In every single election where we're eligible!

Amy: U.S. citizens living overseas can vote. We did—in record numbers in 2018 and, in many races, our votes were the deciding margin to elect progressive candidates.

Sue Ann: Beautiful! One of the reasons I feel so very grateful to you, Bruce, is because even though you moved across the world, you never stopped caring about and for those of us who stayed ... and you are still here beside us, resisting this egregious administration.

Linda: Just to be clear, I wrote this in response to the criticism that those who move overseas have turned their back on their country and don't (or shouldn't) care about what happens back home.

Sue Ann: That was pretty clear to me, Linda. Thank you.

Linda: I wasn't sure—this was written as part of a larger conversation, and I wasn't sure if it was obvious when pulled from its original context. Kinda glad it stands on its own. Thank you.

Tsvika: I think the big flaw in the metaphor, for me at least, is that family is not something you can choose, but your nationality definitely is (or should be). While being born in a family and born in a country are both things out of one's control, family is a construct of people who have consciously chosen to bring another human into the world, whereas a country is a further abstract layer removed. The nihilist in me would argue you should care about your family as little (or as much) as you would for your birth country, but I'm not sure that's a conversation I want to start.

Mark R: I like the healthy distance part. I had a conversation with a British man who was explaining how and why people lose their "right" to vote in England when they have been away. I said we always voted and we always will. That we never stopped being American. I got the impression he thought I was nuts. Not nuts, just patriotic.

Patti: Also don't forget you can still work for causes from abroad. I will still do my campaign volunteer work. To get the voters to the polls.

Luis: We can, and should, be patriotic, even if we recognize right from the beginning that there are serious flaws, both past and present, in our close, loving family. It was never utopian in our family. There are and there were things that we were ashamed of. But we still loved the family and spoke about it and debated these problems and the various possible solutions, and the family listened and tried to improve. Maybe it was that feeling, that knowledge, that certainty, that we were listened to, that we were forging a better future together, that made us love our family in the first place ... together, we were realizing that we had something special and nurturing going on, that even with all our faults, we could be an example for the rest of the community. We were special and we knew it, and we recognized and were humbled by our mistakes, and we were resolute that we would solve them together by using our tools, especially those tools forged in common, based on principle, ethical, righteousness. Thanks, Bruce and Linda, for expressing this so well, and for giving us the opportunity to explore it, add to it, and voice our own feelings on the subject.

Bruce: Thank you, Luis, for contributing so coherently and passionately to this discussion! As a result of this "patriotic" debate, I feel more confident, justified, and comfortable thinking of myself more as an "expat" than an "immigrant."

Immigrants may no longer care about the country they left behind, from which they emigrated. I do. I will always care about the United States of America and a part of me will always abide in that country – voting, volunteering, making my views and positions known, taking whatever actions I can – regardless of where I reside.

Getting a Grip on the Grippe (Gripe)

You know the feeling:

Runny nose. Sneezing. Scratchy or "ticklish" throat. Cough. Watery, tearful eyes. Headache. Fever. Excessive phlegm production. Lack of appetite. Feeling irritable, miserable, overall.

At first it was just a drippy nose, so I assumed it must be allergies.

Even the online weather forecasts here in Portugal and Spain include sections dealing with pollen counts and allergies: "High indoor dust and dander levels," warned today's weather report. Most other days, the level is "moderate," but it's hardly ever really low.

"The problems with suffering from pollen allergy seem to be going on and on this year, and affecting people who have never had this allergic reaction," someone posted in the Andalucia.com forum.

According to the trustworthy Internet, "Inhalant allergies are caused by pollen, fungal spores, house mites, and animal epithelium." Whatever in the world that is, I guessed that our house had it (not to mention all the olive dust circulating from the prolific crop cultivated in both areas where we live).

Whatever "it" is, I was sniffling and wiping a continuously dripping nose ... using up boxes of tissues in the process. Lately, I substituted paper towels for the tissues, as they're more absorbent and longer lasting. Besides, the quality (composition) of tissues sold in our stores here varies substantially from another. Some are almost like the real thing – Kleenex! – yet others are a thin and weaselly wad of waxed paper.

The supermarket's pharmacy recommended Cetinzina. Based on its ingredients, these pills may be Portugal's answer to the USA's Zyrtec, Allegra, or Claritan ... but something very important has gotten lost in the translation.

Not only didn't it work, it didn't help at all.

Don't blame it on the season, friends suggested,

although some equate each with an allergic reaction: "Everything is blooming in the spring." Yes, of course! "This happens every summer" because of all the flies, mosquitoes, insects, and biting bugs. Or, "Why do you think it's called 'fall?' Because everything is falling from the sky and hits you on its way to the ground!" And let's not forget, "It's winter—everyone suffers."

Suggestions for coping with feeling sick because of allergies range from the ridiculous to the sublime:

• Don't go out.
• Don't open any windows or doors.
• Shower and wash your hair regularly.
• Wash clothes and bedding, then dry them indoors.
• What if you must go out?
• Wear a mask, a hat, and sunglasses.
• Buy a car with a pollen filter—then change it regularly.
• Keep only one eye open whenever possible.
• Shove a soft plug of tissue up each nostril. Not pretty, but helpful.

Seriously? For this we moved to Iberia?

Bad became worse last night when, along with other symptoms, I took my temperature and discovered that I was running a 38.5°(C) fever … that's 101.7° (F). There must be something going around in the air here besides allergies and colds, I imagined.

Friends – God bless them! – confirmed my suspicions with a font of facts, figures, and illustrious information:

"Yes, there's a virus going around. I have shivers, can't get warm, feel sick, and my stomach is a mess," shared one. "I had a doctor here about half an hour ago who told me I have gastroenteritis, which is part of this virus (gripe) going around."

"It seems like everyone is getting it: low grade fever, feeling horrible," said another, advising me – as did others – that I could expect to feel awful for the next week … or two.

"If you have a fever, it's the flu."

"I've noticed a lot of people looking like they have the

flu in the past few days" was my favorite remark, imagining how they must look like zombies!

Then came a catalog of tried-and-true remedies and relaxers:

• "Get plenty of rest, drink lots of liquids, and try this recipe ...";

• "If you feel like sleeping, do it. Keep hydrated. Eat if you feel like it; otherwise, have enough so that you don't get weak";

• "Eucalyptus essential oil will help";

• "A doctor has no magic to make it go away—it has to run its course. Watch out for things like pneumonia developing ... it shouldn't, though, if you take care and don't spend all the time lying flat on your back";

• "Paracetamol to reduce fever (don't overdo), chicken soup, fresh orange juice, and lots of bed rest. Keep warm, get as much sleep as possible, and, if it gets worse, do visit a doctor. It could be the real Flu!";

• "It might be the Greep—a pharmacist can help."

And a pharmacist did, with a box of 20 "Trieffect" Antigrippine® to combat the pain, decongest the nose, and lower the fever.

Will it work? Who knows—it has to run its course.

Whether it does or it doesn't, I still intend to follow the advice of a fellow pastor, citing his uncle's all-purpose cure: equal parts of lemon juice, honey, and Old Grandad rye whiskey, taken frequently by mouth.

(The first two ingredients are optional.)

The Emergency Room

Honestly, you don't really know about health care ... until you need it.

It's said that the worst place to be when the flu is rampant is in the emergency room of a hospital.

Nevertheless, there I sat, shuffled from one waiting room to another in Castelo Branco's emergency annex, squeezed into the rear side butt of the hospital, waiting for Russ—or for word about him and his condition.

Russ had been suffering an uncomfortable – sometimes painful – bout with kidney stones for nearly a week. Good luck attempting to see the doctor at your local Centro de Saúde (Tuesday mornings only at ours), or making an appointment with your personal physician ("The doctor can see him a week from tomorrow, later in the afternoon.")

So, there we were at the hospital's emergency room. Trying to explain why we were there to an admitting assistant who spoke not one word of English, nor understood our attempts to describe the situation in our peculiar Portuguese.

"Somos Americanos e não falamos muito português," I explained. Pointing to Russ, I added, "Ele está sofrendo de pedras nos rins."

"Pedras" was a word we knew from the name of a Portuguese soup we've enjoyed very much. And "rins?" According to Google Translate, that's the word for kidneys.

The receptionist asked Russ for his passport and official health number (o número utente). I guess she thought we were tourists, not legal residents, because she handed the passport back when Russ voluntarily passed along his Portuguese residence card. A health insurance card wasn't wanted; with a shake of the clerk's head, it was returned.

After she entered a bunch of information into the computer, we were pointed to the large waiting room and told (in words we did basically understand) to find a seat and wait until Russ heard his name called.

And, so, the waiting began.

About 45 minutes passed (not long, at all, by Portugal's standards), when we heard the ding-dong-ding announcement signal and Russ's name being called.

We stood and walked over to the guard seated on a stool next to the closed door of the sanctum sanctorum. "What do you suppose he's guarding?" I quipped, but Russ was in no mood for jokes. He hurt.

The guard accompanied us to another office at the end of a small waiting room and motioned us to enter. Again, the clerk on duty there spoke little or no English. But she searched for Russ on her computer and output an identification band, which she affixed to his wrist.

Time to be seated (again) and wait some more in a smaller area where the germs seemed closer and more magnified. The place appeared to be more of a "clinic" than what we'd thought of as emergency rooms, its floor littered with tissues and candy wrappers, the anti-bacteria dispenser already quite empty.

Following words muffled too quickly on the public address system, the inside guard – there were two: one on each side of the door – came over and pointed to one of the two examination rooms, where we went. A doctor (we assumed) with short-cropped blonde hair looked up from the paperwork on her desk, waiting for us to explain our presence there—what was wrong?

Russ looked to me, biding me to speak. While we were waiting, I had tried to put the correct words into proper Portuguese sentences, which I then practiced and rehearsed.

"Eeeen-gleesh?" she asked, rejecting my language skills.

"Americanos dos Estados Unidos," I replied.

"I no speak English. Russian, yes. English, não," she stated, as she began a cursory exam of Russ. "Pain? Yes? Não?" she asked, as she squeezed, pinched, and prodded.

After all, she did speak some English!

Following the exam, she led us to a large "treatment" area where people were seated, lying down, or standing—some in wheel chairs, many hooked up to IV tubes. The doctor pulled an already used piece of paper off of a medical exam table and nodded for Russ to be seated. She then directed me back to the waiting room ... the inside one.

About half an hour later, a guard approached and said that I couldn't wait in that room. I understood from what he said that the inside waiting room was for people accompanying patients waiting to be seen by a doctor. The outside waiting room was where you waited, until called inside to be seen by a doctor ... and/or after someone you accompanied had been seen by the medical staff.

Another hour (or so) into my wait, I approached the guard and asked if I could just look in on Russ, so I could make any necessary arrangements. He directed me back to the receptionist—a new and quite friendly one, since a changing of the guard. By spelling his last name, letter by letter in Portuguese, she clicked away on the keyboard, periodically hitting the key to Enter, Enter, Enter.

"Mais o menos outra hora," she informed me, granting permission to bypass the guard and see Russ, who was now sitting in a chair against the wall, an IV tube attached to a vein on the underside of his wrist. They had taken X-rays, he said, telling me he was feeling somewhat better. Who knew what was flowing through that IV tube?

"What now?" I asked. He just shrugged. And I returned to the outside waiting room where I waited some more. Another hour, more or less.

It had been about three hours since we entered the hospital, and I was beginning to become concerned. Did they want to keep him overnight? How were the dogs doing in our absence? Surely, they needed to relieve themselves by now.

I looked up and saw Russ wandering out. He handed me some papers, while he put on and zipped up his jacket.

"The X-rays didn't show anything," he began. "They say I should have an ultrasound test done … but they can't do it here for at least another six weeks, so they told me to go to a private laboratory and have one done there."

"What about these papers?" I asked.

"One is a prescription for pain killers, which we'll need to stop at the pharmacy to get. The other two – including this chart with all the lines – are my vital signs and results of the tests they took."

"Where's the bill?" I continued.

"I don't know."

"Didn't someone give you a bill?"

"No."

Can you imagine being admitted to a hospital in the USA without being asking, first, for your insurance coverage and documentation? Or being treated and allowed to leave without being presented with a bill?

Yeah, right.

We're still waiting for that bill to arrive, perhaps in the mail … now that the kidney stones have passed. It's been several weeks already.

January, First

The day dawned delightful during my early morning walk with the dogs, showcasing Portugal's bluest and brightest skies we'd seen yet in a string of belle weather days. By afternoon it was warm enough not to need a jacket.

Already the sun was rising earlier and the street lights extinguished later, while the town's bells never ceased or missed a beat.

With the help of Facebook to schedule an event and prod people with props and reminders, we had decided to continue our annual tradition of celebrating the New Year with an open house, which we'd combine this year only with a house-warming celebration of our new home here. The last piece of furniture had finally been found and put in place.

We'd be having a "festa!"

Along with wines and beers, lots of different cheeses and appetizers would join our four-food buffet: Pisto, a vegetarian dish I'd learned to prepare from my grandmother in Spain more than 50 years earlier (though I'm told the Portuguese people are familiar with it, too); the quintessential American Mac-and-Cheese, embellished by Russ but done Martha Stewart's way; a new twist on my annual crock pot of Beans and Franks—Beans and Chourizo; and Meatballs served in a special cocktail sauce. Together, they offered an aromatic stew of smells, coalescing to greet our guests: friends old and new.

Side by side, the two crockpots seemed like similes – no, metaphors – of our life now: One, a humble slow cooker with only three basic settings (high, medium, low) purchased from Lidl for 20 euros; the other an oversize, state-of-the-art gizmo with settings galore from Amazon online.

Kind of hokey, huh?

Apart from four of us from the USA, most had moved to Portugal from elsewhere, becoming friends first online or meeting at gatherings with other friends of friends.

Altogether, there were about two dozen of us here ... at one time or another.

More would have come, except that the twelve days of Christmas are counted differently in Portugal and Spain than in the States, going from December 25th through January 5th, the Day of the Magi. Here, people have their own tradition: going elsewhere on New Year's Day.

The concepts of "open house" and "house warming" were new to some of our friends, and foreign to others.

Explaining that we invited guests to visit, at their convenience, between certain times – "stay as long or as little as you choose" – an open house wasn't that difficult to describe. A house warming, however? It simply doesn't translate.

Our Portuguese friends and neighbors, especially, were grateful for the invitation, but felt some hesitation – perhaps reticence is more fitting – about entering houses other than their own to participate in festivities.

These bountiful and gracious people, often poor in pocket but rich in heart and spirit, would knock on our door, dropping off baskets of vegetables and fruits from their quintas.

Despite my limited language skills, I felt confident enough to do the honors by introducing friends and neighbors in Portuguese:

• *Ele é o nosso amigo/Ela é a nossa amiga* (He/she is our friend);

• *Eles são os nossos amigos* (They're our friends);

• *Ela é a nossa vizinha* (She is our neighbor);

• *Eles são os nossos vizinhos* (They are our neighbors); and even

• *Ela é a dona do mini-mercado na esquina* (She owns the little market on the corner).

This is what the good life is about: welcoming people – regardless of who, what, where, when, or how they've arrived – in your lives and being invited into theirs.

Good people. Good times. Good feelings.

Feeling good knowing that you're now in a good place.

Travelogue

Spain is relatively familiar territory.

From our vacation home in Olvera, we've spent time visiting many of the charming "pueblos blancos" (white towns) of Andalucía: Ronda, Grazalema, Pruna, Villamartín, Algodonales, Morón de la Frontera, Antequera, and many others. We've flown into and out of Málaga and Sevilla, passing through this big city on our treks to and from Portugal. We've taken day trips to Granada and Cádiz ... the latter usually to shop at Ikea. Weekend getaways have found us in Martos, just outside Jaén, the provincial capital. Longer vacations were spent in Alicante and the Benedorm playground; later, we disembarked a cruise ship in Valencia.

Attending the University of Madrid for my undergraduate degree, I got to know this special city and notable nearby places: Toledo, Segovia, Ávila, La Granja, Salamanca, and the "casas colgadas" (hanging houses) of Cuenca. During the time of my studies, I traveled to Barcelona, bicycling around this most cosmopolitan city and marveling at Gaudi's La Familia Sagrada. I visited Sitges–one of Spain's first gay destinations during the Francisco Franco regime ... and booked passage on a boat to Ibiza and the Palmas, Mallorca and Menorca.

Portugal is another matter entirely.

It's been nearly a year now since we've moved to our village of Lousa, 20 minutes outside of Castelo Branco. In addition, seeing the sites of this often overlooked city – the Episcopal palace gardens, the white castle for which the city is named, its museums and cultural centers – we've wandered around places outside our own backyard: Alpedrinha, Castelo Nueva, Covilhã, Lardosa, Louriçal, Penamacor, Sertã, etc.

We've have crossed over the awesome aqueducts in Segura on way to and from lunch in Spain ... visited (several times) Monsanto, touted as the "Most Portuguese Town" ... frequented the marvelous Monday market in

Fundão, quite possibly one of the district's best ... feasted our eyes on the spectacular scenery and unparalleled topography of Vila Velha do Ródão and Foz do Cobrão, enjoying the food at one of the best restaurants around.

Now where?

Cutting short our catastrophic "vacation" at a TripAdvisor (aka FlipKey) beach property, we missed out on planned excursions to Porto, Coimbra, Espinho, Tomar, and Aveiro—the "Venice" of Portugal. We'll go back, but we'll do it differently, leaving the dogs at a highly-commended canine "hotel" near us (in Alcains), enabling us to stay at somewhat more comfortable and convenient places.

Also on our list of must-see places is Fátima, as is spending some time in Lisbon – where its expansive aquarium fulfills an exhilarating but exhaustive day – and heading north towards Santiago de Compostela, capital of northwest Spain's Galicia region, for the "Camino" pilgrimage.

But, for now, we wanted to devise a series of day trips ... places within a 90-minute drive ... so we could go, do some sightseeing, and be back in time to feed and walk the dogs. If we were hosting out-of-town guests for a few days, what would we want them to see?

Here are the places on our list:

• **Sortelha** – Somewhat along the lines of Monsanto, Sortelha is one of the oldest and most beautiful towns in Portugal. A visit to its streets and alleys enclosed in a defensive ring and watched over by a lofty 13th century castle takes us back to past centuries among medieval tombs, by the Manueline pillory, or in front of the Renaissance church. Home to the legendary Eternal Kiss—two boulders resting on the slope below the castle walls, just touching, it's not difficult to imagine that they are kissing. Another odd-looking granite formation in Sortelha is referred to as The Old Lady's Head (A Cabeça da Velha). Neighboring town **Sabugal** provides a bonus castle and museum to visit.

- **Belmonte** – Tradition has it that the name of this town in Castelo Branco region's northernmost district came from its location ("beautiful hill"). Near a 13th century castle is Bet Eliahu synagogue and the Jewish zone, with its own special museum.
- **Idanha-a-Velha** – Reportedly invaded and looted throughout history, Idanha-a-Velha is one of the oldest towns in Portugal. Extensive Roman ruins and epigraphs refurbished as a modern museum, a restored 16th century church, and ancient oil press all make this place very special.
- **Penha Garcia** – Situated on a hillside next to the road between Monsanto and the Spanish border, a walk leads up to the castle and a dam below. On the lowest point of the trail, beneath the castle, you can go for a swim in the cool mountain lake. But what makes Penha Garcia truly outstanding is its geology, with huge fossils plentiful.
- **Serra da Estrela** – Even from our lowly house in Lousa, we can see the snow-capped peaks of the highest mountain range in mainland Portugal, whose highest point – Torre, accessible by a paved road – is 1,993 meters (6,539 feet) above sea level. Three rivers have their headwaters in the Serra da Estela, the only place in Portugal during the cold weather to ski, go sledding, snowboarding, or ride a snowmobile. We moved here from Sturgeon Bay, Wisconsin … so, seeing the snow from a distance is quite enough for now.
- **Marvão** – Perched on a granite crag, Marvão is the highest village in Portugal. An old, walled town with gardens and a castle, it's one of the few nearby places included in the *New York Times* #1 bestselling book, *1000 Places to See Before You Die*. Access to the village is through a narrow medieval archway, close to which stands a Moorish-looking building known as the Jerusalem chapel. People tell us that Marvão – deep inside Portugal's hinterland, within a whisker of the Spanish border – is probably one of the prettiest places in the whole of southern Europe because of its views and lunar-like landscape.

- **Piedão** – What could be more romantic than a small town of homes hidden in the middle of the mountains? Astounding architecture attests to mankind's ability to adapt harmoniously to the most inhospitable places, with blue schist and shale houses standing sentry along the sloping terraces between narrow, winding streets.
- **Guarda** – Built around a medieval castle on the northern cusp of the Serra da Estrela mountain range, the dominant 12th century Gothic cathedral is a star attraction and allows you to step onto its roof to survey the city, with a Jewish quarter where Hebrew inscriptions have lasted since the 1100s.

And there's more: **Almeida**, a fortified village whose 16th-17th century castle with all the proper fortifications still remains in tip-top, textbook shape, along with its military museum … **Manteigas**, a glacial valley … Even its name, "Well of Hell," makes **Poço do Inferno** tempting … **Mira de Aire**, with its largest caves in Portugal … **Castelo de Vide's** red-roofed, whitewashed houses clinging to the side of lush mountain slopes and an old quarter described as one of Portugal's best make this small town one of Portugal's gems.

After this bucket list of placeholders has been completed, we can take a train ride on the Beira Baxa line to **Abrantes** in the Portalegre province and visit the 14th century Almeiro do Tejo castle. Will I have the nerve to walk across the castle's steep ramparts—which have no guard rails?

Not even a chance.

Digital Nomads

From dreaming about moving abroad, to researching possible places to live, contacting consulates, asking questions, questioning answers, and getting to know others in similar situations, the Internet – and its social media – is indispensable.

Much of the emigration to Portugal and Spain (other countries, as well) wouldn't be possible without the portability of work and source(s) of income. The Internet makes that possible, creating opportunities to travel, live abroad, and work remotely.

Telecommunications packages are quite reasonably priced in Spain and Portugal—blazingly fast, too, by USA standards. We pay about €50 per month for a plan that includes high-speed WiFi Internet access, two television cable boxes with 200 channels, a "land line" home telephone with free calls, and a 500 MB mobile phone with 2,000 minutes per month.

Most of the people we know who have relocated to Portugal and Spain fall into one of three categories: (1) They're young and resourceful, coming to live on (and off) the land; or (2) Their work is effectively conducted online, regardless of where they live—as long as there's fast, reliable Internet and Wifi available; or (3) They're retired, collecting a pension, and don't give a damn about work.

We've spent countless hours online researching countries and cities, towns, and villages. We read about visa and residency requirements for USA citizens, and studied conditions from health care to real estate.

For those who've asked us where and how to begin, we suggest considering those places where – for whatever reason – you think you'd enjoy living and want to be. Then dive in and begin dredging online. Modern explorers of the digital horizons, you'll be amazed at the new worlds that await you just beyond your computer or wireless device.

Facebook groups have been particularly helpful ...

some are especially informative, while yet others seem more social or geographically-oriented. But you need to be careful: Post the same question to half a dozen groups and you'll be sorting through a mish-mash of confusing and often contradictory information.

Several groups for expats are lively on Facebook. Responsive and capable, I highly recommend these two: (1) Pure Portugal and (2) Americans & FriendsPT. Pure Portugal focuses on the business of buying and selling properties, along with everything that's associated or tangential to the process. Whether its visa or residency requests, health care coverage and driver licenses, different rules apply to Americans (and all those from non-EU nations). Americans & FriendsPT is a most informative and resourceful Facebook community. Questions about matters closer to home? Be sure to join a group supporting your area. Near us are groups for Castelo Branco, Penamacor, Fundão and, no doubt, others. The people who guide and participate in these groups often have the answers you're seeking. You'll also find a variety of buy-and-sell groups for second-hand stuff, if there's something you need or are trying to find.

If Spain is more to your liking, I recommend American Expats in Spain (over 1,800 members) and the Citizens Advice Bureau Spain, a nonprofit organization with a whopping 41,000 associates. With our friends and neighbors, we have Facebook groups devoted to Olvera, Pruna, and What's On In Olvera, Pruna & Algodonales.

Besides Facebook, you'll want to bookmark and use several Google apps. In addition to its powerful search engine, Google Maps is indispensable for its GPS (Global Positioning System) tools. You can drive around areas and look closely at the façades of potential properties and their surroundings, as well as take "test drives" from Point A to Point B (and places between them). Google Translate is another helpful application ... as long as you understand that it's not always accurate. For all the progress and advances Google has made to this product, it still doesn't understand that there are major differences in Latin American Spanish and Spanish in Spain, or that by defaulting to Brazilian Portuguese, it misinterprets the language in Portugal. The biggest problems with Google Translate, however, are correct and appropriate agreement with subject, tense, gender, and number.

More complicated and frustrating than moving to another country on the other side of the world can be adapting to life in a digital divide.

These days, I do less and deliberate more.

I react, pounding out angst and furious frustrations on my keyboard.

Morphing into my computer, I am increasingly dependent on its hard drive and memory for life support. Whatever will become of me if I forget my user name or lose the key password? Access denied!

Facebook has claimed my life, existentially.

Google me.

Best of Both Worlds

It's no secret that we discovered Portugal through Spain.

For ten years or so, we've owned vacation bolts in Olvera, one of the small "pueblos blancos" dotting Andalucía, not far from Ronda, where the provinces of Málaga, Sevilla, and Cádiz collide.

When we decided to emigrate and live our lives in Iberia, naturally we first thought about applying for long-term Spanish residence visas.

However, rather than welcoming our interest and desire to live within its borders, Spain put up roadblocks and obstacles to apply for the visas. After trying to deal with its Chicago consulate, we finally decided that "enough is enough" and considered our options and alternatives.

Friends and neighbors in Wisconsin who moved to Portugal a year before we did advised us, "You really should consider Portugal!"

So, we did.

In the process, we learned a lot about Schengen nation visas (most of the European Union comprises the Schengen zone) and the differences between how one country evaluates immigration visas sought by non-EU nationals and how such requests are handled by other countries.

It's all in the interpretation.

Basically, the components of your visa request – an official Schengen application, FBI background check, confirmed housing, birth certificates and marriage licenses, financial wherewithal, health insurance, etc. – are the same, regardless of which country you're applying to for a visa.

Spain, however, has decided that every page of the documentation you're submitting must be translated into Spanish … and only by a $40-per-page translator on its officially-approved list. (Portugal doesn't.) Spain interprets "financial wherewithal" to mean that an applicant must meet a minimum annual income threshold that the government has set and specific additional amounts for each designated dependent, as verified by Social Security and/or pension income. (Portugal doesn't.) Spain may grant you a retirement visa, but require that neither you nor your dependents work—"*sin fines lucrativos.*" (Portugal doesn't.)

I could continue, but you get the point.

We were made to feel that Portugal wanted us to come and live there; Spain demurred and imposed a lengthy list of criteria and conditions.

So, imagine our surprise when we learned from the Spanish consulates in Lisbon and Porto that simply by going to their offices with our USA passports and Portuguese residency cards (and, presumably, other papers), we could be granted non-lucrative residency status in Spain. Rather easily. Evidently, there's agreement among Schengen countries that, if one grants you residency, it can be transferred to another.

If we wanted, it appears that we could move to Spain and legally live there now full-time. Wasn't that what we had wanted all along?

After Portugal granted our residency visas and first residence permits, we took some time to get settled. About six months later, we went for a month's vacation (and some housework) to our place in Spain.

The differences between the two countries were striking.

While Spain and Portugal can both soothe the soul and lift one's spirit, there's a certain calm and sense of tranquility – a sweet sorrow – that permeates Portugal. There's also a kindred serenity to Portugal, a balm that's conveyed through the least likely of sources: its language!

Despite Slavic-like pronunciation, Portuguese has a softer "shhhhh…" sound than lisping Spanish. It's as if Spanish words were blended, like French, with a sprinkling of something foreign and strangely exotic.

I doubt I will ever master Portuguese or be comfortably conversant in the language, since I stumble over my

Spanish mentality. No matter how I try to understand the rules and logic behind Portuguese, I can't. With rhyme yet without reason, the language makes no sense to me.

But I'll keep trying and working on it.

Because, without realizing how or when it happened, we'd put down roots in Portugal. And language is one of its strongest supports.

Much as we love the place and its people, Spain has always been our home away from home—and it will continue to be … only more often and longer now, thanks to our Portuguese residency.

Maintaining our residence status requires us to spend at least 183 days within a 12-month period in Portugal. Conversely, we can be outside the country for 177 days during this period … a heck of a lot more than the 90 days allowed for USA passport holders to stay in Schengen zone countries.

Yet, who's counting?

POSTLUDE: Retrospective

It's easy to be another one of those Monday morning quarterbacks, but looking back over our life as expats in Portugal and Spain has taught us some incredibly important lessons about things we wish we had known before embarking on this journey.

Sometimes, I still feel as though we're living in a surreal world: a cross between *The Twilight Zone* and *The Fugitive*, with Don Quijote and Alice's white rabbit thrown in for good measure.

Am I actually here, living in a little village of Portugal where I can barely understand the language, expressing myself cogently and coherently? In a land whose food, by and large, I'm not particularly partial to … although its delectable breads, pastries, soups, and wines are among the world's best?

As the first anniversary approaches of our initial residency permits being issued at the SEF (immigration) office in Castelo Branco and we prepare for returning to request two-year extensions, I can't help but reminisce and ask myself what – if anything – we would (or should) have done differently? What nuggets of knowledge or widgets of wisdom might have made the transition from our lives as U.S. citizens in the states to Americans residing abroad easier, quicker, cheaper, more convenient and/or purposeful?

Some things we wouldn't change or do differently. Like shipping our furniture, household items, and personal belongings. Many people leave them behind; we didn't and wouldn't.

Clothing, furniture, textiles and other cherished items collected over the years are often more expensive here. Not only does furniture – especially "good" furniture – cost more in Spain and Portugal than in the USA, but much of what's for sale isn't as well constructed. "Real" wood is a thing of the past and today's furniture is made from chip and particle board or light-weight, balsa-like wood. If you're comfortable with furniture that comes in boxes and is assembled with an Allen wrench per wordless diagrams, you'll do fine. After 30 years of collecting and compiling what we love, we wanted (much of) it to be part of our homes in Spain and Portugal.

Construction brings up the matter of housing and accommodations: Where do you want to live? In a big city? On the coast? A small town or village in the country's interior? Along the border? Surrounded by other expats who speak your language, or as a stranger in a strange land?

Personally, we're not into the bigger places or coastal cities, where prices are skyrocketing because of an influx of "foreigners" buying properties or turning places into profitable Airbnbs, while the natives must flee because they can't afford the inflated prices.

While we love the charm of our little village, it lacks life's provisions only available at stores, shopping centers, and/or large supermarkets. Lousa also comes up short in terms of some of life's conveniences: a restaurant, bakery, pharmacy, hardware store, and lots of other shops.

We find ourselves several times a week in Alcains, a larger town only seven kilometers (not even five miles) away, where all of these niceties and necessities – including our bank and others – are readily available.

All things considered, while properties are somewhat more expensive in Alcains than Lousa, given all our investments in repairs, add-ons, and improvements, the ultimate cost would have been comparable. So, we probably would have purchased in Alcains, instead.

Still might … or even consider looking elsewhere.

You need to do your homework, first online, and then here in person. Spend time in Facebook groups like Americans & FriendsPT or American Expats in Spain. Follow the posts, reactions and responses, carefully. Don't be afraid to ask questions. You will want to be part of an allied community … and it's easier to network, first, online.

Some other suggestions:

• **Spend as much time (and make as many trips) as possible looking at properties and considering locations**. Don't let a property agent sell you on the electricity being off and using a cell phone flashlight to show you around. There's too much hiding in the dark or lurking on the roof and inside the walls that you'll come to regret later if you don't see them clearly and carefully before buying (or renting).

• If you do find a property that you really like, before making an offer – or signing a contract – be sure to **arrange for a "survey" to be done** of it. That's what property inspections are referred to here: surveys.

• Don't be penny-wise and pound foolish. **Think twice – and then, again – about buying a used vehicle** rather than a new one. "Dealers" are legally required to provide one-year guarantees on previously-owned vehicles, but you never know how they'll respond should a problem arise ... especially if that "great deal" came from a purchase not nearby. If the fuel injectors should go kaput where you live, how are you going to get that van back to the dealer for repairs?

• **Consider buying new**. Even in Portugal, where vehicles are somewhat pricier, good deals can be found. Our brand-new Ford Tourneo Courier, for instance, came fully equipped – even with rear parking sensors – and included a seven-year worldwide warranty, for just about €15,000. Similar deals are offered by other brands, too.

• Be sure to **obtain a duplicate copy of your state driving license** before leaving the USA. That's one regret we hear all too often from expats. To get a Portuguese driver license, you'll need to turn in your USA one. After leaving your state, it's difficult if not impossible to obtain.

• Some specialties and items either aren't as cheap or readily available on this side of the ocean as in the USA. Look around at things you use regularly and take for granted. Stock up, especially, and **bring with you small but vital items that don't take up much luggage space**

but will make a major difference in the quality of your lives. Example? Aspirin! Walmart sells 500 low-dose (81 mg) aspirin for just $5.97. In Portugal and Spain, you'll get 90-95 mg aspirin in a box of 30 for five euros—about $5.75!

• Similarly, we wish we'd brought **more pharmaceuticals** with us. Equate 0.5 fluid ounce Restore Tears Lubricant Eye Drops is $1.99 at Walmart. Available only at pharmacies in Portugal and Spain, "artificial tears" costs about five bucks for a smaller size. Prilosec – or its generic, Omeprazole – isn't available in Spain or Portugal without a doctor's prescription, but you can buy 42 tablets at USA Costcos for $13.49.

• **Plastic lids** (can covers or tops) preserve freshness after a can is opened. They're a standard size ... but we can't find them anywhere in Spain or Portugal. Sure, you could use aluminum foil or plastic wrap, but there's something reassuringly uncanny about indispensable and secure lids.

• **Nutritional supplements** like Red Yeast Rice and garlic pills to reduce cholesterol are also hard to find or expensive. A bottle of 1,000 mg garlic pills runs €12 for 90 at the shopping center's health store, vs. $5.94 at Walmart for 200 "softgels," while Red Yeast Rice will set you back €18.27 ($21) online.

• After a good deal of hide-and-seek, we've managed to find most of the grocery items and foodstuffs we use and prefer ... but not crushed red pepper or vanilla extract. Nowhere. Had we known, **a few bottles would discretely have been stuffed in our baggage** between our other belongings. But plain canned pumpkin for the dogs? Forget about it.

• Don't forget that **the move will also impact your pets**. A change in diet and environment is bound to affect them. We have found that adding boiled chicken breast (minced) with lots of cooked white rice – along with tablespoons of freshly stewed squash – to their dry and moist dog food helps them achieve a consistent and productive output.

- Remember that **much will be different over here** than back there. But, that's why you're moving—isn't it? Trust me: You will get used to many things you think you couldn't ... and will even develop a taste for the stronger, more full-bodied coffee!

Scientists say our planet has, maybe, 40 years more. But the dial of the Doomsday Clock shows we're already into the last minutes.

Tick-tock.

Probably the most important difference is our itinerary and timetable: We would have made the move sooner, not waiting so long.

While we will do everything possible, personally and professionally, to make this a more hale and hearty world for all, I have adopted the mantra of Alfred E. Neuman, the cover boy mascot of *Mad* magazine. "What, me worry?" was Neuman's intellectually infamous motto.

Our experiences and escapades, fancies and foibles, over the past year have taught us not to worry so much about the future.

Jesus asked, "Can any one of you by worrying add a single hour to your life?" Looking at the birds of the air, which do not sow or reap or store away in barns, they have food and are cared for, he advised.

Que será, será.

Those words mean the same in Spanish, Portuguese ... and English!

Learning to live them, not just recite them, is part of the mentality we are developing as expats living in Portugal and Spain.

About the Author

Professor, pastor, and author Bruce H. Joffe has amassed an eclectic array of journalism, scholarship, and related experience. Through travel, research and publications, he probes the intersections of media, religion, gender, and other cultural norms—including international living and organized religion. He is indebted – personally and professionally – to Russ Warren … his lifetime partner and longtime companion.